W9-AVJ-921

What people are saying about

The Rise of Lakewood Church and Joel Osteen

and Richard Young

"Once again the Lord proves it is His choice whom He uses. In *The Rise of Lakewood Church and Joel Osteen*, Richard Young documents the miracle that began with a simple man full of faith in the most unlikely location in Houston and reached its apex with the rightful heir in the largest church in America. It is a challenging book that proves radical obedience to the will of God works in the most difficult struggles and greatest opportunities."

—Richard Hogue
Senior Pastor, Citychurch,
Oklahoma City

"Whether you agree or disagree with the ministry of Joel Osteen and the Lakewood Church, you will never see either of them the same again after you read this book. Richard Young has honored both his readers, Joel, and Lakewood in his thoroughness of sharing their amazing story. Even critics will be ignorant about the church and of the issues if they ignore this book."

—Dr. John Vaughan
Author of *The World's 20 Largest Churches, Megachurches and America's Cities*, and *America's Most Influential Churches*, and past president of the American Society for Church Growth

THE **RISE** OF LAKEWOOD CHURCH
AND

JOEL OSTEEN

THE **RISE** OF LAKEWOOD CHURCH AND

JOEL OSTEEN

RICHARD YOUNG

WHITAKER
HOUSE

THE RISE OF LAKEWOOD CHURCH AND JOEL OSTEEN

For speaking engagements, contact:
Richard Young
P.O. Box 272282
Oklahoma City, OK 73137
www.rickyoung.us

ISBN: 978-0-88368-975-2
Printed in the United States of America
© 2007 by Richard Young

Whitaker House
1030 Hunt Valley Circle
New Kensington, PA 15068
www.whitakerhouse.com

Library of Congress Cataloging-in-Publication Data
Young, Richard, 1952–
The rise of Lakewood Church and Joel Osteen / Richard Young.
p. cm.
Summary: "An account of the lives of John and Joel Osteen and their ministry from John's planting of Lakewood Church in a Texas feedstore to its becoming the largest church in America under the leadership of his son, Joel"—Provided by publisher.
Includes bibliographical references.
ISBN-13: 978-0-88368-975-2 (trade hardcover : alk. paper)
ISBN-10: 0-88368-975-8 (trade hardcover : alk. paper) 1. Lakewood Church (Houston, Tex.)—History. 2. Houston (Tex.)—Church history. 3. Osteen, John. 4. Osteen, Joel.
5. Houston (Tex.)—Church history. I. Title.
BX9999.H68Y68 2006
280—dc22   2006031294

DEDICATION

I dedicate this book to two beautiful women who made this book possible:

To my wife, Brenda, whose love and encouragement has made this possible. She reads, "fluffs," and endures everything I do.

&

To Frances Hunter, who has been a friend and source of spiritual support for fifteen years. She is truly an apostle of the faith.

CONTENTS

PART III

THE MINISTRY OF JOEL OSTEEN, LAKEWOOD'S BLESSING

 # FOREWORD

The John Osteen family was and is a very unique family. This is a family that raised their children according to the Word of God. We lived very close to them for many years and never heard one word of gossip about the family throughout all those years.

Dodie Osteen was and is a fabulous mother. All of Lakewood Church has heard her say she never let her children go out of the door in the morning without praying over and blessing them in the name of Jesus. I have heard almost all of her children say the same thing: that their mother never let them out the door without praying for them. I especially remember Lisa saying that one morning, when she was late to school, she was halfway down the block, and her mother was screaming after her, "I bless you, Lisa! I bless you, Lisa!" Whether they were early or late, they always received a blessing.

John Osteen was an incredible father. He always set aside time to be with his children and didn't let anything interfere with that. Joel was very active in all kinds of sports, and John always went to his games during baseball season. John, of course, would always wear his black dress suit. One time Joel said to him, "Daddy, all the other guys' dads wear shorts when they come to the baseball games. Why don't you?" John, always thinking about what it meant to fulfill a desire of his children, appeared at the next baseball game in white shorts. But he still had on his long black socks and black dress shoes.

11

The Rise of Lakewood Church and Joel Osteen

After the game Joel said to his father, "Why don't you go back to your regular suit after this?" I can picture in my mind John Osteen, who was not the shorts type, appearing with the white shorts and the black socks and shoes.

The entire Osteen family live out what they project on television and in their church services. For years we had the privilege of eating lunch with John and Dodie every Sunday. This delightful book shows some of the intimate little details of the Osteen family that you may never have heard. It will delight you. We have known Joel since he was a young boy. We heard him preach his first sermon, and we are there every Sunday to hear his next sermon. We are proud to be members of Lakewood Church.

— Charles and Frances Hunter

PREFACE

From the first time Brenda and I met Charles and Frances Hunter in the early 1990s, they raved about how much they loved Lakewood Church in Houston and their pastor, John Osteen. Although they traveled a great deal themselves, ministering across the nation, they always attended Lakewood whenever they were home. Even when they were on the road, the Hunters would always try to arrive home on Sunday afternoons in time to go to Lakewood's Sunday night service, often driving directly to church from Houston's George Bush Airport. It was due to their excitement for the church that we decided to visit.

From that weekend on, we understood why the Hunters and thousands of others felt so strongly about Lakewood. We began to look forward to returning to Lakewood to hear John preach in person, as well as watching him on television. When John went to be with the Lord in 1999, we joined much of the world in mourning the loss of this great man.

We continued to watch and visit Lakewood whenever we could. The three times we visited Lakewood in 2000, Joel was out of town. We were privileged to hear Brian Houston, from Hillsong Church in Australia, Marilyn Hickey, and Lisa Comes all preach during our visits. We heard magnificent things about Joel, but never heard him preach, except on television. I began work on a doctoral degree in 2002. My doctoral thesis was "The Ten Most Influential Pastors in America." Joel Osteen was among the pastors I listed. When I began the thesis, I decided that if John were still alive he would surely be one of the most influential pastors in the nation. However, since he was gone, I included Joel on the list because of the size of the television ministry and the weekly church attendance, though I did not give him a great deal of the credit. But as I began to make inquiries for my paper, I began to gain more and more respect for Joel and the job he was doing as the senior pastor of Lakewood Church. Each time we returned to the church, we witnessed the growth in weekly attendance that was taking place. The more I investigated Joel and recognized the changes he was bringing to Lakewood, and the growth that was taking place as a result, the more I learned to appreciate him. I soon realized that one chapter on John and Joel's ministry at Lakewood was just not enough to tell the whole story.

My first draft told all about how John built the church—what I thought to be the meat of the story—and ended with a few brief paragraphs stating that Joel had taken over as pastor. I felt the need to add to the chapter, describing the emerging impact of Joel Osteen's leadership at Lakewood. As we continued to visit the church, I began to collect more and more research material, which stretched beyond a chapter and eventually became this book.

In the spirit of full disclosure, I don't deny a strong appreciation for the ministry of John Osteen and the work that Joel continues at Lakewood. I admire a man who was willing to risk his future as an evangelical pastor and step out to become what God intended him to be. I admire a young man who was willing to come out of his comfort zone and follow wherever God would lead. Not many people are willing to do either one. This is the story of what can happen when they do.

—Richard Young

introduction

THE LAKEWOOD
EXPERIENCE

T he experience of going to Lakewood Church begins as
you drive along the various highways around Houston on s Sunday morning. You soon notice that, all
around you, the history of Lakewood is literally displayed on
the bumper stickers of the many vehicles that fill the roads.
These stickers recall various church campaigns from the past:
"Lakewood...An Oasis of Love," "Lakewood—You Were Meant
for Victory," "At Lakewood...Discover the Champion in You."

The closer you get to the Edloe exit, the more traffic begins
to build from all directions. The vehicles vary from Hum-
mers and stretch limousines to older cars that seem to be held
together with wire and duct tape. There are large city buses
filled with people who ride public transportation to church.
Peer inside and you'll often see these people smiling, laugh-
ing, and even singing. You can see the huge, beautiful Lakewood complex from the highway, so by the time you reach the
exit, enthusiasm is high.

When you take the exit, you are directed by police officers
and Lakewood volunteers toward various parking options.
The parking on any particular Sunday morning at the former

stadium is similar to when people attended Houston Rockets basketball games there, except that just before the 11:00 a.m. service you'll have cars coming in for one service and cars going out from the earlier service. And yet, no one seems to mind; all of it only adds to the sense of anticipation. From the time you open your car door, people actually start to enthusiastically greet you. You quickly find that you feel comfortable speaking to strangers, because all are a part of the Lakewood family.

People come to Lakewood from Houston, surrounding areas, and even beyond. It would not be unheard of to meet a farming family from as far away as Oklahoma who attend every other Sunday, except during harvest. If they can't come to Houston, they still attend each week via the Internet.

As you make your way with the crowd, large colorful signs point the way toward Lakewood Church. As you get closer, the frequency of greeters increases. They proudly wear their Lakewood name badges, identifying them by first name. As you reach the entrance you are again greeted with genuine, warm, Texas hospitality—a handshake or hug, and a big "Good morning! Welcome to Lakewood!" It may sound corny, but you have to admit, it really does feel like family.

Just inside are the large escalators, which only go up before services, and only go down after services. At the top and bottom stand eager volunteers who welcome people and assist anyone with special needs. More volunteers are found at the many information booths, areas which were formerly stadium concession stands. Among other things, they offer last week's sermon on DVD or CD and take preorders for today's. They are also willing to answer any questions about Joel Osteen or the many ministries at Lakewood.

Introduction: The Lakewood Experience

They are needed because even if as many as 98 percent of the crowd are regular Lakewood Church attenders, that would still leave eight hundred to a thousand people every week who are visiting and unsure of where to go or what to do. Every Sunday, Joel asks all the visitors to raise their hands, and hands shoot up all over the sanctuary.

As the crowd grows, so does the sense of anticipation. So many people excitedly scurrying about, playing a part in one of the most unique worship experiences in the United States. It's a bit like a Billy Graham crusade service with a charismatic twist, only it happens *every week* at Lakewood!

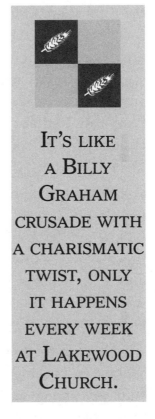

IT'S LIKE A BILLY GRAHAM CRUSADE WITH A CHARISMATIC TWIST, ONLY IT HAPPENS EVERY WEEK AT LAKEWOOD CHURCH.

Upon arriving at the second level, you might drop in on Kidslife, Lakewood's children's ministry. Here, children are enthusiastically greeted by ministry mascots Chase, Kyle, and Champ. Champ has four arms, antennae coming out of his head, and wears tennis shoes. Kyle has blue hair and sunglasses. Chase wears sunglasses, too, and has a backpack and hat. This children's area is nothing like the ones you may remember when you were a kid. The typical dingy, gray classroom walls have been replaced by walls splashed with bright colors and cartoon characters. While you may recall a room with a yellowed picture of Jesus thumbtacked to the wall and water stains from the leak in the roof, these rooms are fresh, clean, and lined with various games and other things you couldn't have even dreamed of as a child. Each room is a theme-filled area with bigger-than-life characters that seem to jump right off the walls. Huge colorful signs indicate the ages for each area, from Baby Builders all the way to The Warehouse, for fourth and fifth grade students.

While you may remember never looking forward to Sundays, for these kids, church is cherished as the best hours of their week. And why not? The moment they enter the Kidslife area, they are greeted by name. Everyone seemed to bubble with excitement, ready to share God's love through a wide variety of fun adventures. And security is top notch: with their state-of-the-art check-in system, they know where every child is at every second.

Having a little time before the service begins, you make your way to the bookstore located on the second floor of the Family Life Center. From one end of the store to the other are Bibles and books in both English and Spanish—including those by Joel himself. There is music, jewelry, and a children's area with Kidslife T-shirts and stuffed animals embroidered with Bible verses. A youth area brims with the latest tools for teens.

Leaving the bookstore, you make your way toward the sanctuary, passing many more volunteers stationed in each stairway to help with directions, information, medical assistance, or any other need that should arise. You decide to forego the main floor and instead choose a seat on the second level.

Once inside, you are immediately aware of an array of blue light. The sanctuary is bathed in a heavenly atmosphere coming from what appear to be clouds with a royal, fine haze

18

behind them hanging above the choir. Such a large space for church may seem a little overwhelming, but you quickly realize that it doesn't really matter where you sit. Each seat has a good view thanks to the large video monitors rising above the working waterfalls beside the stage. Other screens frame the orchestra pit and the choir loft, giving the feeling that you are face-to-face with anyone on the platform. The people around you seem to have developed close friendships with those sitting around them. They must choose the same seats week after week. How interesting for such a sense of community and connection to exist in the midst of such a large and bustling environment.

When the music begins, the crowd jumps to their feet. A live orchestra plays, sounding as professional as any orchestra you've ever heard. Nearby is a lovely African-American lady, dressed in her Sunday best, dancing with her eyes closed, reaching out to God. On the other side is a teenage boy, dancing to the music as if he and the Lord were the only ones there. The crowd is made up of all types: young and old; married and single; African-American, Asian, Latino, and Caucasian. Economic status, race, language, gender—none of that matters when you are bonded in Christ.

In the midst of the music, Joel comes onstage and invites people to come down to the front of the sanctuary for a time of personal prayer. The staff and prayer team are assembling to meet people at the stage and pray for all their individual needs. Prayer team members also appear on the second and third levels of the sanctuary. Pastor Joel, his wife, Victoria, as well as his mother, Dodie, are all there along with the rest of the staff, praying for the needs of anyone who comes down. The time of worship continues as hundreds of people fill the aisles, patiently waiting as everyone with a need for prayer goes forward. It might bring to mind friends of yours who attend much smaller churches—and never even meet the pastor!

When the time of prayer ends, Joel welcomes the millions of people from around the world who are watching on TV to join the service. The uplifting music sets the stage for Joel's message, which works to reinforce the theme that has been communicated during the music and prayer. Then Joel invites those who wish to accept Jesus as their personal Savior to stand and pray a prayer of repentance. Hundreds of people stand throughout the sanctuary. They are immediately handed a packet to assist them in beginning their new life in Christ while Joel shares some wisdom to help them. Then the congregation lets out a cheer as though the Houston Rockets had just scored the deciding points in a championship game. For those who are standing, this moment will be cherished for the rest of their lives. With the help of the orchestra, the choir again begins to praise the Lord for what you have just seen Him do. Everyone stands and, as one, begins to sing in celebration.

With that, the service is over and you look around the room. The people around you are real. They love God and they love each other. Each one represents a changed or impacted life for Jesus, or at least an open and seeking heart. The fact that they attend, or tune in each and every week, is testimony to the fact that they believe that Lakewood is one of the most exciting places to be on Sunday morning.

You realize that there is much more to Lakewood Church than what you've heard people say or what you've seen or read in the media. Lakewood is not just the latest fad.

Introduction: The Lakewood Experience

- Just who is this Joel Osteen?

- What is it about Lakewood that draws people back each week?

- How did Lakewood become the largest church in America so quickly?

Perhaps now your curiosity is piqued and you are eager to learn more about the Lakewood story. Read on...

Part I

THE MINISTRY OF JOHN OSTEEN, LAKEWOOD'S LEGACY

chapter one

GOD CALLS OUT HIS SERVANT

*Before I formed you in the womb I knew you; before you were born
I sanctified you; I ordained you a prophet to the nations.*
—Jeremiah 1:5

The story of Lakewood Church begins with the work that God did within the heart of one man—John Osteen. The Osteen family lived in Fort Worth, Texas, and did not frequent church on a regular basis. John's parents were cotton farmers who had lost everything during the Great Depression, "the poorest of the poor" as Joel has described them. John's mother worked fourteen or fifteen hours a day washing people's clothes for ten cents an hour. On many nights, the family would go to bed without having had anything to eat. John was often sent to school hungry, with holes in his pants and shoes. They were good, honest, hard working folk, but nobody in the Osteen family had ever known any kind of success in life.

Yet God had plans for John Osteen and was keeping an eye on him. When John was only five months old, he jumped out of his sister's arms and into a roaring fireplace. He could easily have died in the flames, but the Lord intervened and spared his life.

25

On another occasion, as a teenager, John was riding the rapids on a local river with friends when his strength gave way. Struggling for air, John went under several times, too weak to cry out to the others for help. Unnoticed, he finally passed out and slipped beneath the steady current. But a boy playing on a log in the middle of the river dove in and accidentally hit John's lifeless form. The boy pushed John into shallow water and was able to revive him. Even in his youth, John was struck by the fact that someone wasn't finished with him yet.

As a child, John had various brushes with the Almighty. He attended Sunday school once or twice. Every once in a while, he was dragged along to a local church service. On one occasion, John recalled the frightening experience of attending a revival service with his mother. The preacher's ominous topic that day was "Be Sure—Your Sins Will Find You Out." Early on, an idea was planted in John's head that he would have to give God an account of his life when he reached the age of twelve. This terrified him and made him dread the arrival of his twelfth birthday, fearing that he would not measure up to the standards of a God whom he did not even know anything about.

In high school, John developed a strong friendship with a fellow student, Sam Martin. The two became best friends. Sam was a "born-again Christian" who constantly spoke to John about his need for the Lord. But Sam was not like the other Christians that John had known. He did not talk about church, the Bible, or the Holy Ghost. He spoke to John about salvation. When the boys had to give reports in school, Sam would talk about Jesus. He was very bold in proclaiming that John needed Jesus Christ as his Savior. Eventually, John became ashamed to be seen with Sam. It got to the point that he would cross the street to avoid him. But the seeds that Sam had planted in John's heart were taking root.

In 1939, seventeen-year-old John was heading home one evening from Lake Worth Casino Beach, a nightclub in south Fort Worth. It was about two o'clock in the morning, and, for some reason, as he walked home John began to think about his eternal condition. He had a desire for God and knew he needed God, but he was afraid to commit his life to Him.

Arriving at home, John began to search for a Bible. He finally found the only Bible in the Osteen home—the big, coffee table kind with family records of births and deaths kept inside. He opened it and began to read, but he really didn't understand it. After a while, he became frustrated and stopped. He stood up and started for the screen door to step outside, but the Lord spoke to him and told him to go back to the kitchen table and open the Bible again. Puzzled, he returned to the kitchen and opened the Bible. There on the pages was an illustration of Jesus standing at a door and knocking. Beneath the picture was a quote from Revelation 3:20, *"Behold, I stand at the door and knock. If anyone hears My voice and opens the door, I will come in to him and dine with him."* After reading it again and again, he went outside and lay down on a quilt. Looking up at the sky, John began to cry out to God, "Oh, God, what will I do when I die? What's going to happen to me when I grow older and go out into eternity?" He thought of Sam Martin and his constant words about the Lord.

As soon as morning came, John called Sam. He told Sam about reading the family Bible, about the illustration and the verse beneath the picture. Sam asked John to tell him what was going on in his heart and mind. Sam then explained, "Why, John, you're under conviction of sin." John wasn't sure what "under conviction" meant, but he did know that he wanted the troubles in his heart to go away. He wanted to settle things with God; he just wasn't sure exactly how to do that.

John pleaded with Sam, "Tell me what to do." His heart and mind were receptive to whatever he needed to do to reach out to God. Sam could hear the sincerity and earnestness in John's voice as he expressed his desire to change his life. As soon as they hung up the phone, Sam went to see John, and together they knelt before God. As Sam led him in the sinner's prayer, John invited Jesus to come into his heart and be his Savior. Sam informed John that he was now saved and that he needed to go to church on Sunday and publicly confess Jesus as his Lord and Savior. Sam reminded John of the many times that he had invited his friend to go to church and he had not shown up. This time, Sam felt that John was sincere and wanted to take the next step in his walk with the Lord. So, they set a date and time to go to church.[1]

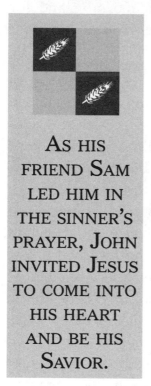

AS HIS FRIEND SAM LED HIM IN THE SINNER'S PRAYER, JOHN INVITED JESUS TO COME INTO HIS HEART AND BE HIS SAVIOR.

When the time arrived, John not only showed up, but he also was there before Sam. When the sermon concluded, the pastor extended an invitation to those seeking salvation. John felt as though his feet were nailed to the floor. He wanted to go forward, he wanted to publicly commit his life to Jesus Christ, but he found himself unable to move. Finally, Sam reached over, placed an arm around him, and said, "John, I'll go with you if you'll go." A little encouragement was all John needed.

Together, the boys walked down the aisle of the church to the altar. The pastor, Dr. Vincent Bennett, asked, "John, will you turn away from your old way of living and confess Jesus as Savior before this congregation of people today?"

John replied, "I don't know. I'm a wicked man; I'm a sinner."

The pastor looked back, smiled, and said to John, "I didn't ask you that. Will you take Jesus as your Lord and Savior?"

John was still uncertain. He told the pastor, "I don't know. I work in the wrong kind of place. I am a popcorn salesman at the Isis Theater in North Fort Worth."

The pastor was still resolute, "I didn't ask you that. Will you accept Jesus into your heart as your personal Savior?"

To that question John's reply was firm, "Absolutely." At that moment his heart opened and received Jesus Christ as his Savior.[2]

John went on to say, "I have come today to give my heart wholly to Jesus. I trust that I can help other young men find Him as their Savior, too." On his way home from church, he pulled off the road at a gas station to pray. He knew deep down inside that something life changing had happened to him that day.

Within three weeks of his conversion, John began preaching the gospel in Southern Baptist churches, on the streets, in schoolhouses, jailhouses, nursing homes—anywhere a crowd would gather. John was very enthusiastic about the gospel of Jesus Christ, but he lacked even a rudimentary knowledge of the Word of God. He mispronounced books of the Bible, such as Psalms and Job. Not surprisingly, everybody around him tried to discourage him. They said, "John, you're never going to make it out there on your own. You better stay here and pick cotton with us. That's all you know how to do. Stay here where it is safe." John didn't listen to them. He responded to the call that God had placed on his life.

A deep desire now resonated in John—to see those around him, including his family and friends, experience God as he had. John had become a new creation; his life in many ways was drastically changed.

> *Therefore, if anyone is in Christ, he is a new creation; old things have passed away; behold, all things have become new.* (2 Corinthians 5:17)

He stopped doing some of the things he had done before. After dinner, when other members of his family went out to nightclubs, John happily sat at the kitchen table at home and read the big family Bible. One night his sister Mary asked, "John, why do you read the Bible instead of going out with us?" Up to this point, John had not spoken to anyone in his family about his experience. Now he sensed that it was time to talk about what had happened. He told her, "Mary, I'll be honest with you. I've let Jesus into my heart. He's become my Lord and Savior. I am through with the nightclub circuit. I'm through living for the world."

Tears began to slip down Mary's face. "John," she asked, "do you think Jesus would save someone like me?"

"Yes, I think He would," John replied. That night, John and his sister got down on their knees, and Mary asked Jesus to come into her heart.[3]

John then began to lead other members of his family to a saving knowledge of Jesus Christ. His father was the big holdout. John's mother had a history of being the one person in the family who occasionally attended church. But John's father never attended church and refused to speak of God in any manner. He was a good father who loved his family, but at no time did he speak to them about a need for God. He would often say, "John, when I'm dead, I'm dead like a dog. Just roll me over in the ditch. There is nothing after this life."

"But, Daddy, it's just not true," John would respond. "The eternal Word of God declares that you are made in the image of God. You will live somewhere. There are only two places to go—heaven or hell. Without Jesus, you'll die and go to hell. I'm not going to give up. I am going to stand for you, Daddy. I am going to go before God and believe for your salvation."

Some time later, John was preaching at weekend revival services at a Southern Baptist church in nearby Dallas. He had asked his mother to bring his father to the services. Watching John preach on Friday and Saturday evenings, his father did not move to do anything. But on Sunday morning, while John was preaching his message, his father suddenly got up from his seat and walked down the aisle. Standing next to his son, he simply said, "I'm going to finish today what I started twenty five years ago. I am giving my life to Jesus Christ." John did not know what he meant by this, but his father explained, "Years

> WHEN JOHN BEGAN TO LEAD MEMBERS OF HIS FAMILY TO A SAVING KNOWLEDGE OF JESUS CHRIST, HIS FATHER WAS THE BIG HOLDOUT.

ago, I got lost in the fields during a snowstorm. I was about to pass out from the cold. I was numb and knew I was going to freeze to death. I couldn't move and I cried out, 'God, if You'll get me out of this, I'll serve You.' Later I woke up as warm as toast. God spared my life, but I forgot my promise."[4]

JOHN'S EARLY MINISTRY YEARS

John understood that he needed some training in the Bible if he was to serve the Lord in the best way that he could. So, in 1943, he enrolled at John Brown University in Siloam Springs, Arkansas, where he earned a bachelor's degree. After graduating, he enrolled at Northern Baptist Seminary in Lombard, Illinois, where he earned a master's degree. During this time, he was also ordained as a Southern Baptist minister.

John's enthusiasm and passion were contagious and he became a very popular preacher. After serving as first assistant pastor at First Baptist Church of San Diego, California, John pastored First Baptist Church of Hamlin, Texas, for three years.

Around this time, John met a young lady and fell in love. After getting married, the young couple worked together in various pastorates, and they were blessed with a son, Justin. The congregations where John served loved him and his young family. But not long after Justin's birth, John and his wife began to experience problems. Their marriage suffered and their problems could not be solved. Eventually the marriage failed.

John was devastated. He thought that his ministry was over, that God's blessings had been lifted from him. He resigned from his position as senior pastor, as well as from the executive board of the church. For the following two years, John worked as a traveling evangelist, holding revival meetings. He knew that he had to quit mourning over what he had lost and get to a place where he could once again receive God's mercy and love. John never dared to dream that marriage and family might be in his future. But God had someone special waiting for him.

Eventually, John was offered another job in ministry, serving as pastor at Central Baptist Church in Baytown, Texas. One day, while visiting a church member, he met an attractive young woman with an unusual first name, Dodie. She was working as a nursing student at one of the local hospitals where John often visited ailing church members. At this point, John didn't know that Dodie was raised in a Christian home and had made the choice to follow Jesus when she was thirteen years old. As a child, Dodie had overcome the terrible disease of polio. She had walked on crutches and had been forced to endure difficult physical therapies. All those hardships played a part in leading Dodie to pursue a career in nursing. She felt a kinship with those who helped others in their times of physical crisis. She had a deep desire to be there for other people.

John fell head over heels for Dodie. He would later say that he knew from the first moment he saw Dodie that she was the one God had chosen for him. John started looking for every possible excuse he could find to go to that hospital. He almost hoped members of his congregation would get sick so that he would have an excuse to go back! Dodie once told her friends, "That minister has the sickest congregation I've ever seen!"[5] The young nursing student still didn't realize that John's secondary motivation was to see her. Eventually, John asked her out and they began to date.

Although John knew very early that he loved her, it took some time before she began to love him in return. While they were dating, they were sitting together under a full moon one night. He was looking at Dodie with eyes full of love, and said to her, "Oh, Dodie, how I love you. I tell you I love you. I wish I had a thousand arms to hug you with!"

Dodie turned to him and said, "I'm not interested in what you would do with a thousand arms. What are you going to do with the two arms you've got?"[6]

Eventually, John asked the former Dodie Pilgrim to marry him, and she said yes. In those early days, Dodie did not know how to cook at all, leading John to often claim that Dodie "couldn't fry water!" In fact, he ate out whenever he could, but wouldn't tell his new wife because he didn't want to hurt her feelings.[7] One time, John got mad at Dodie and decided not to associate or talk with her the entire day. When he returned home, Dodie was hiding behind the door. She jumped on his back as he entered the house, held him around the neck, and yelled, "I am not going to let you go until you give up!" John roared in laughter. As he recalled the story, he asked, "How could I stay mad at the wife that God had given me?"[8]

At the time they married, Dodie was a recent graduate from nursing school, but she knew nothing about being a pastor's wife. Dodie had chosen nursing school assuming that she would remain single all her life. Now, she was afraid that she would not be able to support John's ministry in the way she thought he needed her support. She said to him, "Sweetheart, I can't play the piano. I can't sing. I can't teach a class. I can't do anything a pastor's wife is supposed to do."

John replied, "Dodie, I didn't marry you to play the piano or sing or teach a class. I married you because I love you, and I like you just the way you are."[9] This kind of unconditional love gave Dodie the freedom to realize that she was an original. All her life, God had been preparing her for the call she accepted when she married John, and she would remain faithful to this calling for over half a century.

Today, John and Dodie's faithfulness is most evident in the lives of their two sons and three daughters. Most pastors receive the credit when their children follow them in ministry. But in reality, it is often more due to their wives who have been directing the children in their daily walk with the Lord all their lives. It is often the wives who read the bedtime stories from the Bible storybooks, who make certain the children have evening prayers, and whom the children see as an example of faith on a daily basis. Obviously, John Osteen was a huge and influential presence in the life of his children, but it was Dodie who raised them every day in their walk with the Lord.

John and Dodie were partners in life and in ministry. God had restored John's ministry and had blessed him as a successful Southern Baptist pastor. But John was seeking God in a deeper way—and everything was about to change.

chapter two

THE SPIRIT BEGINS TO MOVE

I indeed baptize you with water..., but He who is coming after
me...will baptize you with the Holy Spirit and fire.
—Matthew 3:11

For some time, John had been reading and rereading the book of Acts. He marveled at the miraculous, supernatural power of God in the lives of early Christians. The more he read, the more he became frustrated; he wanted to see those same things happen again in today's church, and in his life. Throughout Bible college and seminary he had been taught that miraculous signs and wonders no longer occurred. Likewise, the books in his personal library told him that they no longer occurred. Though confused, John continued to minister to the people of Baytown, but because he lacked the spiritual power he read about in the Bible, he only felt more and more frustrated.

John's soul was crying out for a more satisfying experience with God. In the midst of his confusion and discontentment, he made the difficult decision to leave the ministry. He made himself available to preach on weekends or as an occasional fill-in preacher, but in John's mind, his days as pastor of a church were over. He had too many unanswered questions to be a pastor. How could he answer other people's questions when he didn't have answers for himself? John shifted his sights toward a career in business and in making money.

Therefore, following his pastorate in Baytown, Texas, John's calling included a detour into the insurance profession. The business world was an eye-opener for John. He met all kinds of new people as he ventured into his new career. He met professing Christians who used profanity in casual conversation, drank liquor to excess, told off-color stories, and seemed to have no observable spirituality at all. John was astonished. He witnessed Sunday school teachers drunk on cocktails and spewing profanities. They were religious but not spiritual.

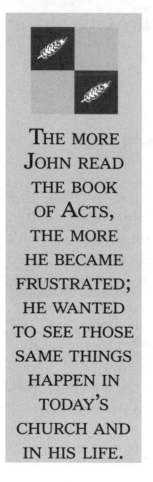

THE MORE JOHN READ THE BOOK OF ACTS, THE MORE HE BECAME FRUSTRATED; HE WANTED TO SEE THOSE SAME THINGS HAPPEN IN TODAY'S CHURCH AND IN HIS LIFE.

One day he was in the office of a man who did not know John was a Christian, much less a former minister. The man was using quite a bit of profanity in his normal conversation. John began talking to the man about his need for a personal relationship with Jesus Christ. The man looked at John with a puzzled look on his face. He pointed to a large book on his desk and informed John that he was the leader and teacher of a deeper life course in his local church.[10]

On another occasion, John was speaking to a man on the telephone. In five minutes he heard the most filthy, obscene language he had ever heard. This was obviously a normal mode of conversation for this man. A few hours later, John attended a dinner meeting at a hotel in Houston and was startled when that same man was asked to pray for the meal. To hear him pray, one would think he was one of the most sincere Christians in Texas. The prayer was a very fundamental, evangelical prayer, and the man closed by calling upon the name of Jesus. Was this what Christianity had become?

John realized that something had to be done about the situation. But as he sought answers, he plainly heard God's voice directed at him, saying, "Well, what have you done? You haven't paid the price to seek My face and find My power." Then God added, "This is the product of the 'easy-believism' that you have been preaching."

At that moment, John took a stand and said, "If no one else does anything about the situation, here stands one man who will." He was determined to set his face toward God and try once again.

Now in his thirties, John accepted the pastorate at Hibbard Memorial Baptist Church, in what would be his last Southern Baptist church. John had read the New Testament and knew in his heart that there was more to the Christian life. He continued to study about those who walked with God in the fullness of power and the Holy Spirit. He did not want just a part of what God had for him; he wanted to walk with God and receive all that God had for him. John later explained, "I can remember when I did not have the baptism in the Holy Ghost. I pastored Baptist churches. I remember that I was doing the best that I could. I felt God in a shallow way, but I had no continuing power. I had been taught in college and seminary that all of this had passed away. That there were no more signs and no more miracles. 'All supernatural things ended when the last apostle died,' they said."

But in his spirit there was a divine dissatisfaction. John cried out to God, "O God, I do not want to die without having had a more fruitful ministry. I want to see more than I have ever seen in all of my life." He described his feelings this way: "I became hungry for more of God. I began to search the Bible. I wanted to satisfy the longing of my heart. In my desperation, I decided to show the Lord I was humble. I said, 'Lord, I am so humble, I will even visit a Pentecostal church.' Such humility! I did visit these people, and they nearly scared me to death. They all started to praise God with such a volume of noise that I thought, 'Lord, surely You are not deaf.' They told me to lift my hands in the air. I got one up, and looked at it. It looked as big as a shovel! When I got both hands up, I felt undressed! They called on me to pray and everyone started praying with me. I couldn't even think about what I was thinking, much less what I was saying! I said, in effect, 'Lord, if You get me out of here, I won't bother these people anymore.' I felt like a Democrat at a Republican convention!"

John preached in his Baptist church on Matthew 3:11, "*I indeed baptize you with water..., but He who is coming after me... will baptize you with the Holy Spirit and fire.*" He told his congregation that he had set his heart on receiving this experience from the Lord Jesus. But it did not come. He found himself in a peculiar situation. He had now told his congregation that he was seeking the baptism of the Holy Ghost; it was on record in front of witnesses. This was a major step for John as he was very active as a pastor in the Southern Baptist denomination, served on committees with other Southern Baptist pastors, and served in various positions within the local Baptist Association. He was on an excellent career path within the Southern Baptist Convention with a very bright future ahead of him.

John was also a man with the responsibilities of a wife and five children. It would have been easier for him to continue on the easy path, causing no spiritual waves. But John chose to step out and seek the power of God with the risk that doing so would end his career with the Southern Baptists. John chose to follow God, wherever that would lead. In doing so, he was placing his life and his family in the hands of God.

John gathered a group of men from the church who were willing to seek God with him. They met early on Sunday mornings and at other times during the week. Together, they cried, prayed, sought, and pleaded for the power of God. Weeks went by and nothing had happened. John had committed himself publicly, but found himself empty-handed in his search for the power of God. He was in "no man's land." He couldn't turn back, and he didn't know what else to do to find what he was looking for. During one service John called on one of the deacons to pray. In his prayer, the pleaded, "O Lord, give our pastor that...that...that, well, Lord, whatever he is seeking, give it to him!"

LISA'S MIRACLE

In the midst of all these changes, both spiritual and professional, something else happened that impacted John's life in every way. Dodie gave birth to a baby girl whom they named Lisa. As a registered nurse, Dodie could tell immediately that something was wrong.[11] The doctor also grew concerned because Lisa did not move properly. X-rays found no broken bones or other maladies, so they released her, and Lisa went home. After several weeks, though, her condition did not improve. John and Dodie took her to a specialist for answers. After examining her, the specialist turned to

Dodie and confirmed what she already knew to be true. "Mrs. Osteen, your child is not normal. She suffered a birth injury and will either be spastic or have something of that nature wrong with her. But she is definitely not normal."[12]

Eventually, Lisa was diagnosed with cerebral palsy. Her color was strange, and she had no muscle tone in her body.

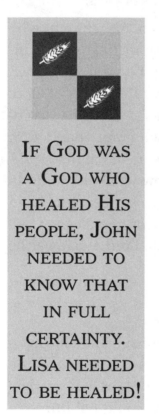

IF GOD WAS A GOD WHO HEALED HIS PEOPLE, JOHN NEEDED TO KNOW THAT IN FULL CERTAINTY. LISA NEEDED TO BE HEALED!

She had no sucking reflexes and was not able to lift her head from the bed, even a fraction of an inch, until she was five months old. She didn't have the strength to crawl. The doctors told John and Dodie that she would never walk and would probably need twenty-four-hour care for her entire life. The prognosis was bleak and there appeared to be no hope on the horizon.

John and Dodie needed a miracle! John retreated to his office at the Baptist church and closed the door, leaving instructions that he was not to be disturbed. Day after day, he was alone with the Word of God. In his heart he said, "I don't care what college and seminary professors taught me. And I don't care what dark tradition says. I am going to take the Word of God and I am going to find out what God has to say to us about our baby."

John was still the pastor at Hibbard Baptist Church, leading people with no tradition or understanding of a God who could heal the sick. John himself knew very little about God's power and desire to heal His people, but Lisa's illness had

John focused as nothing else in his life had ever done before. If God was a God who healed His people, John needed to know that in full certainty. Lisa needed to be healed! If God was truly out of the healing business, then John would do whatever he could do in his own strength to help Lisa. But if God could and would heal, then John would call on Him with all his might until Lisa received her healing.

John began to read through the four Gospels. He read the accounts where Jesus healed the sick while He ministered on earth. Over and over again, he read the promises of God to heal the sick. In a time of crisis, many people get angry with God and turn away at the very time they need to draw near to Him. In the midst of their crisis, instead of running from God, John and Dodie ran to God. John discovered the God of the Bible in a fresh way—as a loving God, a healing God, a restoring God, and a God of miracles.

From the Word of God, John and Dodie learned that the miracle they were looking for was in their mouths! Not only did they need to believe the Word of God, but they also needed to confess the Word, out loud! Each day John and Dodie lived with the promises of God from His Word.

> *He sent His word and healed them, and delivered them from their destructions.* (Psalm 107:20)

> *Heaven and earth will pass away, but My words will by no means pass away.* (Matthew 24:35)

> *Forever, O LORD, Your word is settled in heaven.* (Psalm 119:89)

Days turned into weeks, weeks faded into months, as they stood fast on the promises of God to heal Lisa. Dodie's nursing experience told her that if Lisa did not sit up alone by the seventh month, it was a sure sign of abnormality. Dodie watched as the fifth month came and went. Then the sixth. The last critical days for Lisa to sit alone were speeding by. Then something happened: Lisa turned over and was able to sit up all by herself.

God is a God of healing! Healing had not passed away! It was for today! Jesus had touched baby Lisa! From that day forward, Lisa developed normally. Doctors confirmed her complete healing. (Today Lisa often preaches to the congregation as an associate pastor at Lakewood.)

The experience with his baby daughter changed the ministry and message of John Osteen forever. John began to focus on the God who wants to help us instead of the God who wants to sit in judgment of us. Seeing the heart of God for the first time, John began to preach of the goodness and love of God, instead of the anger of God. John began sharing with his congregation that we are to come to God so that we can embrace the God who loves us, not so we can avoid the judgment of a vengeful God. Through the healing of Lisa, not only had the life of one family been powerfully impacted by God, but now thousands of people's lives were to be touched by this loving God.

Having witnessed the healing power of God firsthand, John was determined to experience all that God had promised. John would describe this experience of waiting upon the Spirit as "tarrying." Jesus had told His disciples,

Behold, I send the Promise of My Father upon you; but tarry in the city of Jerusalem until you are endued with power from on high. (Luke 24:49)

During John's several weeks of tarrying, he began to understand Scripture as he had never understood it before. Traditional teachings he had learned in college and seminary were challenged as John began to believe in something called the baptism of the Holy Spirit. He asked the Holy Spirit to search and show him everything that needed to be taken care of so that his heart would be pure. The Lord reminded him about bills he needed to pay, restitutions he needed to make, and wrongs that he needed to make right. John was swift to obey the Spirit. He corrected things as promptly as they were brought to his attention. When all the obstacles had been cleared, the Lord started the work in John that He had intended.

One of the things that John learned, and would later teach his congregation, was that there are no shortcuts with the Lord. Many claim to want all that the Lord has for them, but at no cost to their lives and their relationships with others. But in Scripture John found that there is a price to be paid. And he was willing to pay any price and go any distance to be certain that there was nothing stopping him from receiving what the Lord had for him. He knew that if there was anything the Lord revealed to him that he was not willing to do, correct, or rectify, then Jesus was not his Lord.

As John renewed his efforts to seek the face of God, he found that God began to honor those efforts.

One night, in his office, John had an encounter with God. He was sitting and quietly praying before going home. Suddenly a feeling much like electricity came over his hands. It began slowly, but increased in intensity until it felt like multiple volts of power were surging through his hands and down into his wrists. His hands were actually drawn up in the air by this power. Then he heard a voice in his heart that seemed to say, "Lay these hands on the sick and they will recover."

He had never had an experience like this in his life. He was frightened and not certain about what had actually happened. In desperation John called a friend. Not sure what to think about John's story, the friend took John to the home of the Reverend J. R. Goodwin, an Assemblies of God minister. The Goodwins prayed and laid hands on John, praying for him to receive the Holy Spirit. Right there in their den, John began to speak words that he could not understand. Rev. Goodwin also spoke words that were equally unfamiliar.[13] John was so unnerved with all the noise they were making that he did not feel at liberty to release himself. Rev. Goodwin explained to John that he had indeed received the baptism of the Holy Spirit and spoken in another language, an unknown language. John had heard the strange words that came out of his mouth, but he thought it must have been of his own initiative and not from God. He was not convinced. He wanted to know without a doubt that what he had received was from the Holy Spirit of God.

All his life, John had been taught that it was important that he maintain control at all times. When he spoke those strange words, he knew that he was definitely not in control. But it was not yet settled in John's mind just who was in control. Was the Holy Spirit in control? Or was it something else?

John returned to his office full of doubt. The devil seemed to be saying to him, "That was just you talking. You did not receive the Holy Spirit."

For several days, whenever he prayed, the same few words kept coming out of his mouth. John shook his head in wonder. Determined to settle the issue once and for all, John checked into a hotel room. From his rented room in downtown Houston, John cried out to God, "Oh, God, the hour is late, hell is too hot, heaven is too real, eternity is too long, and my responsibility is too great for me to fail You in this hour. I want all of heaven, all of hell, and all of creation to witness that I am willing to reach this generation by Your supernatural power."

The Lord replied to him, "Are you willing to be numbered among the despised and those who are ostracized? Are you willing to lose the prestige of your denominational standing... to be fired from your church and have your salary cut off? Are you willing to have every door shut against you and never be invited to preach in their churches again? Are you willing to be ridiculed and embarrassed because people look upon you as a fanatic?"

To all of these questions and many more John cried out, "I am! I am! I am!" John raised his hands to heaven and the Lord began to do a work in him unlike anything he had ever experienced. John basked in the glory of God's power as it poured in like a raging stream from heaven for a long time.

When John had gone to the hotel room, he had told Dodie that he did not know when he would return. She thought he would be gone for several days. But after just a few hours, John called Dodie and told her that he had received the baptism in the Holy Spirit in all its fullness. "Tell me about it," she said. John was hesitant to describe everything that had happened over the telephone. He knew that she was seeking the touch of the Lord in the same way that he had been, and he wanted plenty of room for Dodie and him to rejoice in the

Lord together. John was confident that God would meet the desire of Dodie's heart and fill her with the Holy Spirit. Shortly after John's hotel visit Dodie received her own visit from the Holy Spirit.

John assumed that others would rejoice at his breakthrough, as Dodie had. But that was not to be the case.

chapter three

GOD IS AWESOME, BUT NOT EVERYONE BELIEVES

And no one puts new wine into old wineskins; or else the
new wine will burst the wineskins and be spilled, and
the wineskins will be ruined.
—Luke 5:37

When John received the long-awaited baptism of the Holy Spirit, various members of his Baptist church rejoiced with him. They were happy that the hunger in his heart had finally been fed. People filled Hibbard Memorial Baptist Church to hear John tell of what the Lord had done in his life—and that He could do the same for them. The Holy Spirit was new and fascinating to them. During this time, more and more people came to Christ and were saved as John talked about Jesus hour after hour. Many also received the baptism in the Holy Spirit.

However, there was another group within the church who were not pleased. Such workings of the Holy Spirit were not consistent with their Baptist doctrine or tradition. Yet, despite the presence of such skeptics, miracles began to occur at Hibbard Memorial. God was doing things that no one had ever seen in this church or anywhere else.

One Wednesday night it seemed that Jesus Himself walked into the church. A little girl who was crippled sat in the front pew every Sunday. Everyone knew the little girl and was aware that her foot and ankle were crippled. Her ankle was as stiff as steel, requiring her to wear a built-up shoe. As rivers of miracles began to flow that night, the strong presence of God touched the little girl, and her ankle popped loudly. Instantly, she was healed.[14] News of the healing spread rapidly. Such an inexplicable phenomenon stirred up all those who were opposed to this new movement of the Holy Spirit in their church. It was becoming apparent to the dissenters that, if something was not done soon, they could lose control of their little Baptist church.

Even John's sermons began to change. He now spoke of a loving God, rather than a God of judgment and condemnation. He spoke of a heavenly Father, rather than a judge who was demanding and impossible to please. John taught that God wanted them to be healthy, happy, and whole. Some responded to this movement of the Holy Spirit and experienced a hunger in their hearts for more of God. Many of them received the baptism of the Holy Spirit, while others received healing. Prayer meetings at the church went on all night long, with folks coming and going at all hours of the day and night. All in all, about ninety people came to a full experience of the power of the Holy Spirit. They were a sight, this small group of happy Baptists, speaking in tongues and always talking about Jesus.

But a larger group of others remained on the outside, watching and wondering what it was all about. This group began to fight for control of the situation; they intended to make certain that their church would remain as it had been before. Gossip began to spread. "Brother Osteen has started giving people drugs to make them happy. No one has any right to be this happy all of the time. Surely he is giving them drugs." Others were saying, "Brother Osteen is hypnotizing the people." Others warned their children to stay away and not get caught up in it. The new wine of the Spirit was bursting the old wine-skins.

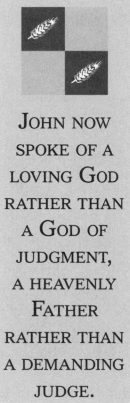

One cool, rainy night John was called to visit a woman who had had a death in her family. She was to leave the next day to go to a distant city for the funeral. After talking with her for a while, they prayed together, and John stood to leave. She said to him, "Wait a minute, Brother Osteen. I have some coffee and cake for you." As she started to stand, she grabbed her knee and groaned in pain.[15]

John now spoke of a loving God rather than a God of judgment, a heavenly Father rather than a demanding judge.

"Are you sick? Do you need prayer for your body?" John asked. Always eager to pray for the sick, John habitually kept a vial of oil with him so that he could anoint people and pray.

She said, "Oh, Brother Osteen, I have arthritis throughout my entire body and I hurt so badly. I've had it for years. Look at my right hand. It is so stiff."

John looked at her hand and noticed that the place between her thumb and index finger was completely hardened. There was no movement in that area of her hand. John asked her,

"Please let me anoint you with oil and pray for you." She agreed, so he anointed her with oil and prayed.[16]

After prayer she went to get the cake and coffee and they sat and talked some more. As John got up to leave again, she grabbed her leg and groaned in pain. John said to her, "Oh, do you still hurt?"

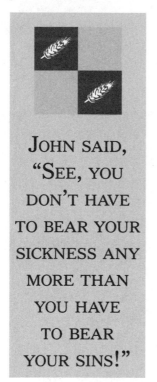

JOHN SAID, "SEE, YOU DON'T HAVE TO BEAR YOUR SICKNESS ANY MORE THAN YOU HAVE TO BEAR YOUR SINS!"

Not wanting John to feel discouraged, she said to him, "Brother Osteen, it's not your fault! You did all that you could do. It is not your fault that I still hurt!" She knew that he had just started praying for the sick and that, historically, Baptists did not know much about healing. Then she said something that revealed the path to her healing: "Brother Osteen, the Lord expects us to suffer some."

John said, "What did you say?"

"The Lord expects us to bear some of our pains."

The excitement in his voice became evident as John said, "Did you know that Jesus not only bore our sins, but that He also bore our sicknesses too?"

She replied, "Why, no, I didn't know that!"

John hurriedly got his Bible and turned to Matthew 8:17. He said, "Look! Look! Read what the Bible says!"

She read, *"That it might be fulfilled which was spoken by Isaiah the prophet, saying: 'He Himself took our infirmities and bore our sicknesses.'"*

John said, "See, you don't have to bear your sickness any more than you have to bear your sins!"

She began to shout with joy, which scared John, who had never seen a Baptist woman shout like that. He said to her, "What's the matter?"

She told him, "When I read that Scripture, all the pain went away!" Then she freely moved her hand and said, "Look at my hand. I can use it. I can use it!" In a moment of time, she was completely healed.

MINISTRY CONFRONTATION

Hibbard Memorial Baptist Church quickly divided into two camps: those who believed in the supernatural power of the Holy Spirit, and those who did not believe and wanted things to remain as they had always been. Not only did some individuals within the church find the changes offensive and inappropriate, but denominational officials were beginning to question the changes in John's church and ministry as well. Eventually, Southern Baptist officials in Texas announced their intention to try John for heresy.[17]

Being a Baptist church with congregational governance, the members took a vote to determine whether John should remain as pastor. A majority of the voting membership backed John and gave him their support as pastor. But the dispute was far from over.

During the next few months, some of the people of the church treated John very badly. Those who had lost the vote were not satisfied with the outcome. If they could not vote him out, they were determined to run him off. They refused to respect him as pastor and as a man of God. Disappointed and brokenhearted by their behavior, John finally decided that the best course of action would be to let them have their church and move on.

In the fall of 1958, John Osteen resigned from Hibbard Memorial Baptist Church. For a few months, he tried his hand at a business career, but it soon became apparent that this was not the plan that God had for him. He was not happy and longed to follow the calling of God on his life. John knew that God was calling him to start a whole new church.

chapter four

HOUSTON AND
THE WORLD

Go into all the world and preach the gospel to every creature.
—Mark 16:15

O n Mother's Day, 1959, John and Dodie Osteen welcomed ninety people to a dusty, old, converted feed
store on the northeast side of Houston—and Lakewood Church was born. Many of these people had made the
move from Hibbard Baptist Church. Legend has it that the
slats of the wooden floor of the building had such large holes
in them that people sometimes lost their money to the ground
below during the offertory. Lakewood was an independent
Baptist church that embraced the full gospel, including heal-
ings and speaking in tongues. Not long after the church
started, a storm blew through, taking the word *Baptist* off the
sign and leaving only the words *Lakewood* and *Church.* John
took it as a sign from God that they were never meant to be
a Baptist church and left the name as God had changed it—
Lakewood Church.[18]

John's very first message was entitled "No Limits." He
wanted everyone to know that there were no limits to what
God could do in the life of anyone totally given over to Him.
There should be no limit to where a Christian is willing to go to

reach others for Jesus Christ. Lakewood Church saw the world as their mission field. John was determined not to fall into the traditional religious "ruts." Before he was Spirit-filled, he felt he was caught in such a trap—the trap of having to meet the expectations of men rather than God. John was determined to do things God's way, regardless of what any man said or thought.

Eventually, John came up with the slogan that would one day be plastered on thousands of bright blue bumper stickers all over Houston: "Lakewood Church, an Oasis of Love in a Troubled World."

From the very beginning, Lakewood was unique. Worshipers sang and praised the Lord with joyous enthusiasm. They felt free to cry out to God during services, fall down on the ground and shake with excitement, or publicly testify how the Holy Spirit had healed a physical illness. But perhaps the most unusual aspect of Lakewood Church was that, in Texas in 1959, a white man opened a church in what was—and still is—a predominately African-American neighborhood.

John welcomed anyone who wanted to worship God, including the area's African-American families. He figured that God saw no skin color, so why should Lakewood? And the families of the area came. They first came out of curiosity, to see the small white man who dared to start an integrated church in their community. But those who first came out of curiosity stayed at the little feed store church because of the love of Jesus.

God had led John to start such integration within the church before the civil rights battles of the 1960s. He may have been small in physical stature, but John became a giant when he was led by God. Little did he know that more than forty years later Lakewood Church would still be one of the few fully racially integrated congregations in the United States, all because of John's desire to share Jesus with everyone and anyone. Today Lakewood's congregation is about forty percent white, thirty percent black, and thirty percent Hispanic.

Over the next several years, John and Dodie were faithful to serve the Lord in this unusual church. But God had an additional plan in store for John—the call of God to reach the world.

LAKEWOOD TAKES OFF

When word got out that a former Houston Southern Baptist preacher had been baptized in the Holy Spirit, many invitations to speak in various places all over the country began arriving. John was anxious to share this truth: that God was able to touch the lives of people everywhere through His power and through His Holy Spirit.

In order to communicate what God had done in his life with as many people as possible, John rented a school auditorium in Pasadena, Texas. It was the perfect location—close enough to draw people from Houston, yet far enough away so as not to attract negative attention from his former denominational ties. The meeting was widely promoted. John was enthusiastic about what God was going to do during the services. Hundreds of people came from all over the area. Many came expecting a move of God unlike anything they had ever experienced. They desired to see miracles happen under the power of the Holy Spirit. Others came expecting to mock their former denominational comrade, hoping he would fail in front of a large crowd of people.

When the big night arrived, John began by enlightening the assembled crowd about his Southern Baptist background. He spoke of how he was now filled with the Holy Spirit and shared how he had discovered that the gifts of the Holy Spirit are to be experienced in the lives of all believers. At the end of the service, John took a bold step of faith by announcing that they would see miracles in Jesus' name that very night. He invited those who were in need of prayer to come forward. A line formed at the platform and ran down the steps and curved into the aisles of the auditorium.

As the first person walked across the stage, a hush came over the auditorium. It was a thirty-year-old, mute Spanish man who had never uttered one word aloud in his life. This was a true challenge of everything John claimed to believe. The naysayers were excited; this was what they had come to see. Surely John would be proved a fool when this mute man would be unable to speak. John thought to himself, *Oh, God, why couldn't I have started with something like a stomachache?* With butterflies in his stomach, John stood over the mute man and commanded the demon to come out in the name of the Lord Jesus Christ. John placed the microphone to the man's mouth and told him to say, "Thank You, Jesus."

The once mute, Hispanic man clearly spoke into the microphone the English words, "Thank You, Jesus." The meeting exploded with the power of God! Many were saved and baptized in the Holy Spirit. Others received great miracles. Only the critics left disappointed.[19]

After this, John was used of the Lord in many services across the nation. What would be known as the charismatic movement was only just beginning, and John was one of a group of people whom God called out of mainline and evangelical denominations across the country and pulled into the fullness of the Spirit. There were others. Dennis Bennett was called out of the Episcopal Church. There was an assortment of fellow Southern Baptists, such as nationally known youth evangelist Richard Hogue, and the founder of Church on the Rock, Larry Lea. Men like John Wimber and Chuck Smith would step out of their comfort zones to receive all that God had in store for them. In the early 1960s, there was also a charismatic movement at some Roman Catholic colleges.

John Osteen found himself on the cutting edge of this great move of God. Leaving the security of a denominational organization and either becoming part of a denomination open to the fullness of the Spirit or becoming an independent church was a very frightening thing. But through the example of John and others, many were encouraged to step out and accept the full power of God.

JOHN OSTEEN FOUND HIMSELF ON THE CUTTING EDGE OF THIS GREAT MOVE OF GOD.

John was ministering all over the country, holding healing services and encouraging everyone he could to receive the power of the Holy Spirit. Along the way he grew in the power of the Lord and experienced other gifts of the Spirit firsthand. Often, he received a word of knowledge about someone in the audience having a certain ailment and needing a healing touch from God. He learned to walk in the prophetic, interpreting a word in tongues or giving a word from God in tongues. He shared with others about the things the Lord had told him. This was a time of tremendous spiritual growth for John.

By the mid-1960s, John felt a definite calling from the Lord to go to foreign lands. This calling was confirmed through the actions of others who offered to help him. Responding to the call, John visited many countries and developed a real passion for the lost of the world. God gave him a real love for the nation of India. He also had a special place in his heart for the Philippines. John would keep this passion for the rest of his life. When the Lord touched this Baptist preacher, He gained an obedient servant who would follow Him anywhere and everywhere He would ask him to go. It has been said, "The world has yet to see one man totally sold out to God." John Osteen came close to being that man.

chapter five

MARY'S MIRACLE

Do not be afraid, Mary, for you have found favor with God.
—Luke 1:30

One person who had a tremendous impact on John's life and ministry was his sister, Mary Givens. Mary joined the Hampton Baptist Church in Dallas, Texas, where she was dedicated to God and serving Jesus with all of her heart, actively teaching a Sunday school class at the church for many years. Having a soulwinner's heart, her class had to be divided again and again because of its growth due to her powerful teaching.[20]

After several years, Mary began to experience severe seizures. A neurosurgeon in Dallas ordered a brainwave encephalogram and other tests, which confirmed that Mary was afflicted with epilepsy. Later, John would say that he did not believe it was epilepsy; he believed it was the devil.[21]

Mary was sucked down into a dark hole as she slowly began to lose her sense of reality. At first, she struggled to recall Scripture that she had memorized. Eventually, she couldn't even remember the name of God. Treatment began immediately with Dilantin, a small pill she had to take two times each day. Mary was cautioned against ever missing it, even for one dose. After nine weeks on the medication, Mary was able to concentrate, study, and even to teach again. But

Mary's health then began to slip as horrible nightmares, black-outs, loss of memory, and stumbling necessitated further treatment by other specialists. For a time Mary improved and tried to go forward, but she soon recognized the changes in her own personality and behavior. She now withdrew from family and friends whom she had always cared for. When the phone rang, Mary would not pick it up, either because the pain in her head was so intense, or because the voice on the other end of the line would inevitably say, "Mary, you don't sound like yourself." She wanted to scream, "I'm not myself! Help me, someone!" She knew she needed help, but she didn't know where to turn.[22]

Eventually, Mary fell into a coma-like state in which she did not open her eyes for two weeks, even amidst all the frenzy of the hospital. Doctors reported that an infection had set in within her brain, the cause of her latest seizures. Mary endured months of suffering from violent attacks on her mind and body. For many years Mary was in and out of hospitals and institutions, even enduring shock treatments.[23] Finally, Mary was sent home with no hope of recovery. There was nothing more that could be done for her. She was unable to walk, her equilibrium was gone, and she could not even feed herself or go to the bathroom. Mary now required around-the-clock nursing care.[24]

At this time, John was totally unaware of her condition. Mary had not seen her brother in over two years. They had been very close, but family and ministry responsibilities had caused them to grow apart. As John was driving down the East Texas Freeway in Houston, his sister came before him in a vision. It was not an open vision but a strong spiritual perception. John turned to Dodie and her mother, who were in the car, and said, "Mary is terribly sick, but the Lord just told me she shall be delivered!"[25]

Two days after the vision John's mother called to tell him that Mary was indeed very sick. John responded, "Mother, I know all about it. God spoke to me that the hour of her deliverance has come."

She began to cry, "John, how soon can you come to Dallas?"

"Mother," John replied, "Dodie is in the hospital. I want to be here until the baby is born."

That night, after the baby was born, John left Dodie and their newborn and drove to Dallas. He fully understood that the situation was bigger than he could handle on his own. Before starting his car John placed his hand on his Bible and asked God to speak to him about Mary. As he opened his Bible, his finger landed on Luke 1:30 and the words of the angel Gabriel, *"Do not be afraid, Mary, for you have found favor with God."* The Lord was even mentioning Mary by name! John prayed in tongues the entire 240 miles from Houston.[26]

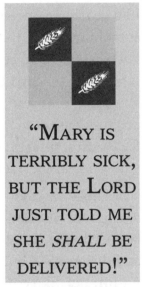

"MARY IS TERRIBLY SICK, BUT THE LORD JUST TOLD ME SHE *SHALL* BE DELIVERED!"

When John arrived in Dallas, he went into Mary's house accompanied by the Reverend H. C. Noah, pastor of Oak Cliff Assemblies of God Church. Mary did not recognize John or Rev. Noah when they entered the house. But she did hear someone saying to her, "Get out of bed!" Before she knew it, she was standing on her feet, falling in every direction like an infant taking her first step.

Together, John and Rev. Noah were praying and defying the evil one who was in the room trying to destroy Mary as they supported her attempts to walk. The two men informed the destroyer that they knew the truth: that God could and would set her free. They declared it done, pointing to the cross and claiming its power for healing and for the defeat of him who had dared to intrude on God's territory. Mary heard her brother's voice as they laid hands on her head and prayed in tongues. For several days she had not heard anyone's voice clearly, but now John's voice began to penetrate her mind. It was as though she was in a fog. Mary heard a language she could not translate, but it did not seem foreign to her. It was like hearing a once-familiar voice that she had forgotten. Mary somehow knew that the voice was saying, "The victory has been won." A voice instructed her, "Rise up and walk." And when Mary heard the voice of God speak, she did not walk, she ran! John and his mother were jubilant! Mary walked around the room and talked to everyone. She ate solid food for the first time in days. Later she would tell her husband that she sensed that she was shut up with God.

Those around her noticed that the glazed look in her eyes was gone. Her love for God and for all those around her was restored. She did not sleep for two days. It was not that she could not sleep, but the energy and Spirit of God were strong within her. She could sense the ongoing presence of the Lord in the room. With spiritual ears, she could hear music coming from the portals of heaven. When Mary stood and walked for the first time after her illness, she was also filled with the Spirit with the evidence of speaking in tongues. For several days after her healing, John stayed and taught her from the Word of God.

chapter six

GOD BLESSES LAKEWOOD

But he who received seed on the good ground is he who hears the word and understands it, who indeed bears fruit and produces: some a hundredfold, some sixty, some thirty.
—Matthew 13:23

Through the decade of the 1960s, John continued to speak across the nation and throughout the world. He preached in crusades, held training classes for pastors and evangelists, and touched thousands of lives everywhere he went. He made friendships and built relationships with people around the world. Back home in Houston, Lakewood Church was growing ever so slowly. For the entire decade, Lakewood continued to meet in the feed store where the church was founded. John served as an interdenominational missionary from 1961 to 1969. During this time John would often leave Houston on a Monday morning, go to a foreign country to minister for several days, return to Houston on a Saturday, thirteen days after he left, and then preach on Sunday morning. In his absence, an associate pastor, Marvin Crow, would fill in for John, ministering to the needs of the Lakewood congregation. Crow was a good and faithful servant of the Lord, but he simply was not John.

Dodie worked at the church as well, but she had five children at home and was busy keeping the home together.

While ministering in the Philippines, God spoke to John very clearly and told him that it was time to return to Houston and take up the ministry at Lakewood. John obeyed this call and returned to full-time ministry at Lakewood in 1969.

John would continue to reach out to foreign countries from time to time, but for the rest of his life the focus of his ministry was on Houston and Lakewood Church. Lakewood would go on to send millions of dollars in support of international missionaries, Bible schools, orphanages, and medical clinics. John would continue to visit the mission fields around the world and preach there as he could. He would always have a passion for the nation of India. He wanted to visit and preach there again, even to the day he died. But he understood the voice of God and obeyed.

Lakewood Church did not become a megachurch overnight. The church maintained an attendance in the area of two hundred for well over thirteen years. This was a dry season for John in many ways. A fellow minister asked him, "John Osteen, what are you doing pastoring this tin feed store with these few people?" John's response was that he was doing what God had called him to do. Others said to John, "You should be evangelizing around the world. You should be on the other side of town. Why don't you move to the good side of town?" But John stayed where the Lord had placed him.[27]

In order to grow, the church needed more land. As soon as eighteen acres became available next to the church, John contracted to purchase the land for two hundred sixty-four thousand dollars. Then one day, as John was driving down the road, the Lord spoke to him very clearly. He told John not to buy the property, to lose the five-thousand-dollar down payment if he had to, but to get out of the contract. John quickly called the church treasurer, and they negotiated a release from the contract, forfeiting half of the five thousand dollars. Perhaps the Lord knew that a recession was coming that would drive the price of real estate down in Houston. Perhaps the Lord knew that two years later Lakewood would be able to purchase the same eighteen acres for sixty-seven thousand dollars. John's obedience to the Lord's urging saved Lakewood nearly two hundred thousand dollars. It also gave John another example of God's desire to lead His people in a supernatural way.

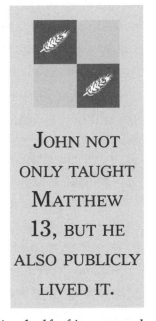

JOHN NOT ONLY TAUGHT MATTHEW 13, BUT HE ALSO PUBLICLY LIVED IT.

John made it clear to his Lakewood congregation that God wanted His people to plant a seed in the ministry of Lakewood Church and that God wanted Lakewood Church to plant seeds in ministries all over the world. It was not uncommon for the church to give half of its annual income to world missions. John would verbalize their goal, "To reach the unreached and tell the untold." He began to teach his congregation to speak and confess the Word of God. In the church services John would have the people make bold confessions aloud in unison, "My house is paid for. My cars are paid for. All my bills are paid. I don't owe anybody anything. I have money in the bank. I am not stingy. I am not covetous. I am evangelizing the world." Once the Word of God reached down into their hearts, the church began to grow and God blessed it in every way. As a result of their unified confession, one by one their homes were paid for as God honored their faith.

This was a dramatic change from the Southern Baptist traditions John had taught in the past. Prominent teachers and pastors in evangelical and mainline denominations rarely taught such a doctrine. Speaking and confessing was strictly the territory of the Pentecostal or charismatic movement. John invited such men as Oral Roberts and Kenneth Hagin to come and speak at Lakewood Church. This was viewed by some, then and now, as controversial.

John not only taught the doctrine of Matthew 13, but he also publicly lived it:

Then He spoke many things to them in parables, saying: "Behold, a sower went out to sow. And as he sowed, some seed fell by the wayside; and the birds came and devoured them. Some fell on stony places, where they did not have much earth; and they immediately sprang up because they had no depth of earth. But when the sun was up they were scorched, and because they had no root they withered away. And some fell among thorns, and the thorns sprang up and choked them. But others fell on good ground and yielded a crop: some a hundredfold, some sixty, some thirty. He who has ears to hear, let him hear!" And the disciples came and said to Him, "Why do You speak to them in parables?" He answered and said to them, "Because it has been given to you to know the mysteries of the kingdom of heaven, but to them it has not been given. For whoever has, to him more will be given, and he will have abundance; but whoever does not have, even what he has will be taken away from him. Therefore I speak to them in parables, because seeing they do not see, and hearing they do not hear, nor do they understand. And in them the prophecy of Isaiah is fulfilled, which says: 'Hearing you will hear and shall not understand, and seeing you will see and not perceive; for the hearts of this people have grown dull. Their ears are hard of hearing, and their eyes they have closed, lest they should see with their eyes and hear with their ears, lest they should understand with their hearts and turn, so that I should heal them.' But blessed are your eyes for they see, and your ears for they hear; for assuredly, I say to you that many prophets and righteous men desired to see what you see, and did not see it, and to hear what you hear, and did not hear it. Therefore hear the parable of the sower: when anyone hears the word of the kingdom, and does not understand it, then the wicked one comes and snatches away what was sown in his heart. This is he who received seed by the wayside. But he who received the seed on stony places, this is he who hears the word and immediately receives it with joy; yet he has no root in himself, but endures only for a while. For when tribulation or persecution arises because of the word, immediately he stumbles. Now he who received seed among the thorns is he who hears the word, and the cares of this world and the deceitfulness of riches choke the word, and he becomes unfruitful. But he who received seed on the good ground is he who hears the word and understands it, who indeed bears fruit and produces: some a hundredfold, some sixty, some thirty." (Matthew 13:3–23)

One Sunday morning John got up and announced a special offering; however, it was not for the new building for Lakewood, but for the small Spanish church down the street that was also in the midst of a building program. Several thousand dollars were collected in that offering, and a check was sent down the street to the Spanish congregation. Lakewood needed the money as much as the Spanish church did, but John believed in the Matthew 13 principle. He knew that Lakewood had to get some seed in the ground. He lived by this principle: In time of need, sow a seed. He believed one of the best things he could do in a time of famine was to plant some seed. It wasn't long after planting that the seeds began to grow. Lakewood now had all the money that was needed to start work on the building project.

John wanted to be an example to his congregation and family in every way. Integrity was vitally important to him. Not wanting to give the enemy any opportunity to use his life to ridicule the faith, John did all that he could to live blameless before the Lord.

Around this time John suddenly grew very ill. A group of doctors examined him and discovered that he desperately needed open-heart surgery if he wanted to live a long and healthy life. The entire Osteen family was in shock. John loved his family very much, and he loved the work he did for the Lord. He had constantly preached about a God who healed His people. John did not want anyone to doubt the healing power of God on his account, so he examined his heart and his life to see if he had overlooked anything spiritually that needed to be made right, and he took steps to resolve any issues between himself and anyone else. After a heart-searching self-examination, John decided to follow his faith and not have the open-heart surgery. He told his doctors that he was going home. He was placing his life and body squarely in the hands of the Lord.

LAKEWOOD EXPANSION

With John fully focused on the work at Lakewood, the church began to grow rapidly. In 1972, they built a simple but more substantial building than the original feed store, seating seven hundred—and they did it debt free. In 1979, the church building was expanded to seat three thousand, on folding chairs. This remained their home until 1988 when Lakewood constructed a one hundred twenty thousand-square-foot sanctuary in East Houston seating eighty-two hundred.

John was always sensitive to the timing of God when building. This was especially the case when beginning their 1988 church building. Joel would later describe it this way: "For many years my dad tried to build this sanctuary. Things weren't coming together and we put it on hold. Two or three times he announced to the congregation, 'This fall we're going to break ground for a new sanctuary.' Fall would roll around and he would say, 'It's just not the right time.' Daddy had enough sense to wait for God's perfect timing."[28] Renee Branson, Pastor John's secretary for seventeen years, said, "God told him two things. 'If the people tithe and give over and above, then the buildings will be debt-free.'"[29]

During the Christmas season of 1986, in the midst of one of the most severe recessions that Houston had ever experienced, John instructed the people to be faithful to the Lord and give out of their abundance. But he knew to wait for God's timing. On February 15, 1987, the church broke ground on the new building. Construction began in April and was completed eleven months later. The entire 5.2-million-dollar cost of the project was raised before the building was completed. Four weeks before the dedication service, John asked anyone who could give a thousand dollars toward erasing the final half-million dollars to come forward. About two hundred people approached the stage. The following Wednesday night, without John asking anyone, people spontaneously stepped forward with cash and checks for an hour. And all this was at a time when fifty-two banks failed in Texas, twelve of them in Houston.[30]

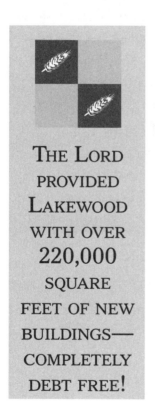

THE LORD PROVIDED LAKEWOOD WITH OVER 220,000 SQUARE FEET OF NEW BUILDINGS— COMPLETELY DEBT FREE!

The new auditorium was dedicated with much fanfare. The mayor of Houston, members of Congress, Word of Faith evangelists from all over the country, and missionaries from fifty-eight countries were present. Billy Graham sent a videotaped message, and President Reagan sent a message as well. The dedication of the building coincided with the eighteenth Church World Conference hosted by Lakewood. Thirteen hundred missionaries from around the world were in attendance. They heard some of the best-known evangelistic speakers in the world, including R. W. Schambach, Oral Roberts, Kenneth Hagin, and T. L. Osborn.

In 1991, a thirty-seven thousand-square-foot children's addition was completed. Then the Lord told John to build an educational and office building in one year, and to pay cash. And not only that, the Lord instructed John that he was not to take a single special offering for the building. He was to tell the people to give above and beyond their tithes, as the Lord would lead them. The sixty-two thousand-square-foot, three-story educational and office building was completed in 1993, with the cash raised in one year. As these building projects were completed, people grew in their faith. In view of the fact that they witnessed the Lord doing amazing things in their midst, they learned that they could believe Him for anything. In a seven-year period of time, the Lord provided Lakewood with over ten million dollars and built over two hundred and twenty thousand square feet of new buildings with twenty acres of parking, and everything was completely debt free!

John and Dodie Osteen personally conducted Lakewood services right up to the 1990s. Before many churches had a band, Lakewood knew you could have more than an organ in a church service. Dodie would lead the entire service, including taking the offering. Following the music, she would invite anyone who needed prayer for physical healing to come forward. As people came forward, Dodie, John, and other Lakewood prayer warriors prayed for their recovery as they laid hands on them and anointed them with oil. After everyone who desired prayer had received, John would take the pulpit and preach the Word. John never ended a service without issuing an invitation for lost souls to come forward and meet Jesus Christ as their Savior.

Lakewood Church was host to many well-known evangelists during this time. In 1987, when Oral Roberts made his controversial remarks about the Lord taking him home if sufficient funds were not raised for the medical school at the university in Tulsa that bears his name, he came to Lakewood to speak and raise funds. John and Dodie stood beside him during this time. They had been friends for some years and the Osteen's son, Paul, was a graduate of the ORU medical school.

Early in 1988, Pat Robertson visited Lakewood during his presidential campaign, where he addressed thirty-five hundred people, drawing the attention of the Houston media. John welcomed him to Lakewood although, following his normal practice, he refused to endorse any particular candidate for office.

Later in 1988, televangelist and Word of Faith proponent Kenneth Copeland spoke at Lakewood in a major conference called the Houston Victory Campaign. Copeland's ministry was known as Voice of Victory.

At that time, Lakewood had one of the largest auditoriums in the country. John Osteen was well known around the world because of the national television ministry Lakewood had begun. He was also known as a man of unimpeachable integrity. John's endorsement to a ministry and his friendship with those in ministry was something to be cherished. All of the large charismatic ministries went through Lakewood hoping to receive John's approval and support.

"SEVEN YEARS OF HARVEST"

In 1994, once all the buildings were built, John announced a major campaign of giving to missions—"Seven Years of Harvest." This cause was closest to his heart, and he urged the people to give as much as they could above their tithes. John worked harder at this giving campaign than at any other time he raised funds. He set a goal to raise twenty-nine million dollars for missions during the seven years of harvest. This was more money than was raised to build all the buildings combined, and it was a great deal more than most small denominations gave to missions.

John preached a series of sermons on giving as part of this campaign. The series was a part of every service Lakewood had, Sunday morning, Sunday evening, and Wednesday evening. John repeatedly told people that if they were faithful to God, He would reward their faithfulness. He used every verse in the Scripture he could find that would teach the people that God wanted them to be blessed financially. John wanted to show them that God would take the seeds they planted, their tithes and offerings to missions, and give them a harvest of thirty, sixty, and even a hundredfold.

In every sense of the term, John had the heart of a missionary. If God had allowed him, John would have spent his life preaching and teaching to the people of the world. But God called him to build Lakewood to become one of the great churches in the world. Through Lakewood, God used him to touch the world with his international television ministry and the financial gifts of the people of Lakewood Church.

John informed his people over and over where and how the money would be spent. He told them of supporting native pastors in Asia. He brought them up-to-date regarding the presentation of *The Jesus Film* to villages around the world that had never heard the name of Jesus Christ. He told them of the number of sermon tapes that were being sent all over the world. The people of Lakewood were continually being reminded of how they were making a difference in reaching the world. John told the Christian world through the weekly television broadcasts that Lakewood was going to touch the world for Jesus Christ. The campaign was to last from 1994 to the year 2000. Although John would not to live to see the end of the "Seven Years of Harvest" Campaign, it was successfully completed in his memory.

Of course, there was more to Lakewood Church than physical buildings and Word of Faith conferences. As the church multiplied several times over, members got to know each other by involving themselves in all kinds of ministry. More than thirteen hundred people worked in ministries ranging from outreach to sailors at the Port of Houston to ongoing Bible study and counseling projects with hospital patients, school students, and gang members. Many volunteers worked as greeters and ushers in the church. Everyone was welcomed into God's house when they walked into Lakewood. Rich or poor, black or white, young or old, speaking Spanish or English, everyone who walked into a Lakewood service felt he or she had come to a real "Oasis of Love." People got involved in everything from service and hospital ministries to street evangelism; members still head downtown each week to try to win souls for Jesus. The church cooperated with other ministries that reached out to the hurting and needy of Houston with food and clothes. There were a host of ministries to help those who attended the church but found themselves in need.

Racial diversity continued to be a hallmark of Lakewood. John's sermons were translated into Spanish for the Hispanic community, who could also listen to simultaneous translation of the service through a low-power FM signal within the church. The church bookstore had a strong selection of Spanish materials, and many of John's books and tapes were also available in Spanish.

Lakewood Church continued to try to meet people at the point of their need. Whether the need was for food and clothing or for spiritual-growth materials in a foreign language, Lakewood was driven by a love for people. There was no doubt that everyone was accepted at Lakewood Church, regardless of status or race, and that there would be an attempt to meet the needs of people whenever those needs were indentified.

chapter seven

DODIE'S BATTLE

Bless the LORD, O my soul, and forget not all His benefits: who forgives all your iniquities, who heals all your diseases.
—Psalm 103:2–3

By 1981, many things were happening in the lives of John and Dodie Osteen. Their youngest son, Joel, was turning eighteen. With many of their children either in college or grown, the Osteens were making plans for the future. John and Dodie were invited to be special guests at the dedication of the Oral Roberts City of Faith Medical and Research Center in Tulsa where their son, Paul, was a student at ORU's medical school. The first day of the dedication was a great time of celebration, but later that evening, Dodie began to experience chills and a fever. Over the next three weeks, her symptoms grew progressively worse until, eventually, she was unable to sleep and became jaundiced. Still, throughout this time, Dodie worked hard to maintain the ministry activities as she always had. At one particular service, she knelt to pray for a lady but found that she was so weak she could not get up. She crawled to a chair and pulled herself up. But not even Dodie knew how sick she really was.

Around this time, preparations were being made at Lakewood for a Thanksgiving convention. John and Dodie talked and decided she should go to a doctor to make certain she was able to fully participate in the meeting. They called The City of Faith and were referred to a specialist in Houston. After examining her, the doctor ordered Dodie into a hospital for some more tests. Dodie asked if she would be going in as an outpatient so she could attend the meeting. The doctor told her that the tests would be much more extensive and would require more time and care.

Expecting a brief two- or three-day stay, Dodie did not know she would be in the hospital for twenty days! The initial diagnosis was an abscess on her liver. She received treatment, but the medications had side effects of nausea and depression. Further tests, however, contradicted the first diagnosis. Finally, the doctor came into her room and told her that for his own peace of mind they were sending some blood work out of state for tests to rule out a malignancy. Dodie called John in shock. She did not want to even utter the word *cancer*. They agreed to stand together against even the possibility.

On December 10, 1981, John was entering the hospital to visit Dodie when the doctor met him in the lobby. He told him that Dodie had metastatic cancer of the liver and that, with or without chemotherapy, she had only a few weeks to live. Treating her would only prolong her life for a short time, so the doctor asked for permission to do exploratory surgery or a colonoscopy, as they had not yet located the primary tumor. After considering this, John told the doctor, "I am going to take my wife home. We are going to pray and seek God, and then we will decide what to do. We believe in miracles, and we believe in the Miracle Worker."

"Well, Pastor," the doctor replied, "you are going to need a miracle this time."[31]

John went to Dodie's room and told her of the doctor's diagnosis. She was shocked but sat quietly and listened. Their son, Paul, was doing his surgery internship down the street at another hospital. John called him and asked him to join them in Dodie's room. Paul had been observing while his mother had been in the hospital and knew that something was horribly wrong, but when he heard the diagnosis, he began to weep. He knew that God could heal, but he was also well aware of the prognosis for someone diagnosed with liver cancer—there was usually not much hope. Dodie encouraged her son that he was going to have to help her fight this. From then on he was a strong supporter.

Dodie and John decided to put her life in the hands of the Lord. That day, amidst Houston's busy rush hour traffic, John drove Dodie home from the hospital.

In the Hands of the Great Physician

Friends from around the country began to call. Oral Roberts, T. L. Osborn, and Kenneth Hagin called. Daisy Osborn came to Houston to pray for Dodie. The people of Lakewood were fasting and praying. The family was staying strong. One night, in the early hours of the morning, Dodie sensed the voice of the Lord saying, "It is not your husband's faith; it is not Oral Roberts's faith; it is not Kenneth Hagin's faith; it is your faith that you must rely on now." From that moment, Dodie realized that her healing would be a personal matter between her and Jesus.

Once she got home, she never took to bed to be cared for by others. She felt that doing so would demonstrate unbelief and undermine her faith. She went to bed only during her normal sleeping hours. She did not even take a nap. The first morning home, she got up, bathed, and put on a dress that swallowed her now eighty-nine-pound frame. She was not going to act sick. That first morning she told John, "Darling, you are the head of the house. You are going to have to take authority over this cancer in my body. We must agree that God is going to heal me and make me whole." John anointed her body with oil and they both got on the floor in the bedroom, facedown before the Lord. John took authority over any disease and over any cancerous cells in her body. That was December 11, 1981, the day Dodie's healing began.

Despite continued suffering, various symptoms, and still feeling ill, Dodie knew in her heart that her healing was underway. In the middle of the night, she would plead her case with the Lord. Her family needed her. The church needed her. The Lord needed her. She examined her heart as God began to deal with her about some things. One night she wrote letters to seven people whom she felt she might have offended, whom she needed to forgive, or who needed to forgive her. She wrote letters to people she thought she might have offended after she had become ill and became irritable. She wrote a letter to each of her children and one to her husband. She did anything she could think of to help her maintain a positive, helpful attitude. By her bed, she placed a picture of herself in her wedding dress. Her wedding day was one of the happiest days in her life and she wanted to be reminded of happier times. She then placed another picture of herself riding a horse when she was on vacation. She wanted to picture herself healthy and happy.

Dodie searched the Scriptures and found every verse in which the Lord proclaimed that He was a God who wanted to heal His people and make them well. She would read those

Scriptures every day before leaving the house and keep them close to her during the day. She would fill her mind with the verses before she went to bed so that, as she slept, the truth would be in her spirit. She used them to build and retain absolute faith in her healing.

She forced herself to get out of the house and pray for others. She did not feel like going out, but when she stayed at home she felt her health decline. She was putting her faith in action. Every day Dodie left her house and ministered to others. As she did so, she gained hope and encouragement from the promises of God.

She clung to the Word every day, reading and confessing the Scriptures. She bathed herself in the Word of God. There were times when she felt herself wavering. There were days when she wouldn't feel well, and she wondered if it was just normal illness or something worse. She spoke to John about this concern. She asked him if something was wrong with her because of her doubts.

DESPITE CONTINUED SYMPTOMS AND STILL FEELING ILL, DODIE KNEW IN HER HEART HER HEALING HAD BEGUN.

His response was direct: "Dodie, are you wavering in your heart?"

She responded, "No, I know God's Word wouldn't lie to me. It's true."

He asked her, "Then, where are you wavering?"

She considered for a moment and then replied, "In my head."

John said to her, "Well, don't you see? That's the difference. You are not wavering in your heart, because you know God's Word is true. There is no need for you to be condemned. Your heart is established. Resist the thoughts from the devil, and he will flee from you."

Dodie realized that she had faith in her heart, but doubts in her mind. Later she would be able to teach others not to condemn themselves when they doubted in their minds. The important thing is to keep our faith strong in the power and might of the Lord and we will see His power manifested in our lives. Dodie has been an inspiration to people around the world who have suffered from cancer. They see her standing in front of the congregation of Lakewood as a visible testimony to everyone about the power of God to heal His people.

In November 1983, a full two years after she received the death sentence of cancer, Dodie had some blood work done. She went to Dr. Reginald B. Cherry, a doctor of preventive medicine and a member of Lakewood Church. The test results confirmed that God had performed a miracle. The blood work was totally normal. Seven liver function tests were completely normal. There was no cancer at all. God had performed a miracle in the life and body of Dodie Osteen, and the doctor confirmed it.

The daily healing verses that Dodie used were eventually made available to others through several booklets at Lakewood. She continues to quote those verses to herself to this day. She knows that it is not only important to maintain her faith, but that she must also do everything she can to maintain her healing.

Years later, John and Dodie were talking together regarding her healing. She asked him, "John, why did God decide to heal me when so many others have died of cancer?"

John said, "Dodie, God didn't choose to heal just you. God has chosen to heal everybody."

"Well, why was I healed?" she asked.

John said, "Because you decided to take God at His word."[32]

John and Dodie believed and taught that God is not a respecter of persons. Healing is for everyone. Salvation is for everyone. God does not play favorites.[33]

Part II

Times of Transition

chapter eight

LAKEWOOD TAKES TO THE AIR

Behold, I will do a new thing, now it shall spring forth;
shall you not know it? I will even make a road in
the wilderness and rivers in the desert.
—Isaiah 43:19

I n 1983, John's youngest son, Joel, was a student at Oral Roberts University. He had always had an affinity for marketing and often wondered, *How do we get more people to come to Lakewood?* The answer seemed obvious—television. Joel later said, "I think the possibility of going into someone's living room, in their own environment, it's such a great tool. When Coca-Cola wants to reach a generation, they go to TV and the people are watching."[34] Joel called home from Tulsa and told his father that he had an idea. Even though he was only a freshman, Joel wanted to drop out of college, go back to Houston, and put Lakewood Church on television.

John was always open to new ways to reach people for Jesus. He agreed to his son's plan, but with one stipulation: Lakewood Church would never use the cameras to ask for money. Joel eagerly agreed and moved back home to get started. He immersed himself in getting Lakewood's message of Jesus to millions. He quickly found out that there was a lot of work involved in starting a television ministry, and a need for a lot of money for the proper cameras and equipment. At that time, Lakewood was not a large church. It did not function on huge budgets or benefit from members with great fortunes. But it was a place with a lot of faith. For several months, John laid out the vision and put his faith into action.

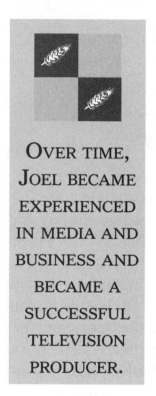

OVER TIME, JOEL BECAME EXPERIENCED IN MEDIA AND BUSINESS AND BECAME A SUCCESSFUL TELEVISION PRODUCER.

Every service he stood up in front of the people and announced that Lakewood was going to start a television ministry as soon as God provided the money for the equipment.

One Sunday, John received a note during the service. A man in the congregation had come to church for several weeks in order to receive prayer for healing. John didn't want the man to wait another minute. He went to the pulpit and asked the man to stand up in his pew so that he could be prayed for wherever he was in the auditorium. The man stood in the back with great difficulty and began to walk forward on crutches. He had endured five back operations and, as a result, one of his legs was drawn up and did not touch the floor.

With excruciating pain, he inched his way toward the platform. John tried to dissuade him by saying, "Just stay where you are. There is as much of the power of God in the back of the auditorium as the front." But the man kept inching forward. John spoke louder, thinking the man might not have heard him, but the man kept coming forward. The moment that the man reached out and touched the stage, the Lord touched his body. Immediately, this crippled man began to praise the Lord and run around the auditorium. People in the congregation began to shout and praise God all over the auditorium. Then a prophetic word came forth: if the television ministry had been in place, this miraculous healing would have been witnessed by the whole world instead of just the church.

Now the people of Lakewood put their faith into action. One million two hundred fifty thousand dollars in cash and pledges were collected for a television ministry in that one service.[35] In the midst of God's supernatural power, the television ministry of Lakewood Church was born.

By the mid-1980s, Lakewood was broadcasting locally on KHOU-Channel 11, Houston's CBS affiliate, to sixteen cities across the United States, as well as to Brazil and the Philippines, and on the Christian Broadcasting Network, a national cable network. And leading this ministry from the control booth was Joel Osteen.

Behind the scenes was the perfect role for Joel because of his eye for details. While taping one of the services, Joel noticed that John's suit, tie, and shirt were not very photogenic on the television cameras. Wanting his father to look his best on camera, Joel started making a trip to his father's closet every Saturday to pick out his father's wardrobe for the following day. Joel and John worked side by side to edit and produce the television show. Over time, Joel became experienced in media and business and became a successful television producer. As Lakewood's television program achieved a global outreach, Joel's talent for marketing also helped Lakewood reach out to all of Houston. If one were driving on a Houston freeway, it became hard not to see John Osteen's smiling face shining down from strategically placed billboards about town. The *Houston Press* asserted that the Lakewood jingle, "We believe in new beginnings, and we believe in you," ranked as one of the most successful marketing campaigns in Houston's history.

Channel 55

In the late 1990s, Joel and his wife, Victoria, were presented with an opportunity to go deeper into the television ministry with Charles and Dowan Johnson. The Johnsons were father and son ministers from Conroe, Texas. Since 1980, they had been trying to secure the license for Channel 55 in Houston. Finally, in March of 1998, Joel and Victoria joined the Johnsons as the station's new owners.

On July 15, 1998, Channel 55 went on the air as the eighteenth broadcast station in the Houston market and the last possible UHF station to launch. From the beginning, it was announced that Channel 55 was to be a family-style entertainment format. The first vice president of the station had previously worked with the Family Channel. True to Joel's marketing skills, the station had a brand from the beginning. It was called "The Tube." It signed on at six o'clock in the morning with a devotional.

Neither John Osteen nor Lakewood Church had any kind of financial investment in the new television channel. The *Houston Chronicle* reported that the source of Joel's funds for the station came from a local bank.[36] It was the decision of the four owners that Joel would serve as the station president. Joel quickly honed his team-building skills as he began to assemble the Channel 55 team. Joel's staff consisted of Mark Reiff, who had extensive experience with the Houston TV sales market; Wendell Burton, former advertising director for the Family Channel; and Victoria's brother, Don Iloff, as vice president of marketing and communication.

Eventually, Lakewood announced that it would be changing its local broadcasts of services to Channel 55. When questioned, Joel said the move had less to do with his owning the station than with the decision of Channel 11, the previous location for the Lakewood broadcasts, to add football games to their schedule during the Lakewood time period.[37] Channel 55 announced a schedule of religious broadcasts from six to noon and from ten to midnight on Sundays, as well as six to seven each weekday morning.

When his father passed away, there were rumors that Joel would sell the station. There had been offers for the station, especially since the FCC had changed the rules to allow ownership of more than one television station in a given market. But Joel announced that he would still be involved in the major decisions regarding the station; however, Matt Reiff would handle the day-to-day operations.[38]

GOD PROVIDED JOEL WITH THE KIND OF LEADERSHIP DEVELOPMENT THAT HE WOULD NEED VERY SHORTLY.

In October 2000, Joel hired a new general manager for the station, saying that his new responsibilities at Lakewood limited his time and focus. The station was adding local programming; it became the new television home for the Houston Rockets of the NBA and for the Houston Comets of the WNBA, requiring the station to increase its production staff.

When the opportunity for Channel 55 presented itself, Joel was in his mid-thirties and already the leader of his father's television ministry. Many people in his position would have been too overwhelmed to even consider such a possibility. But Joel and Victoria had always expected God to do great things in their lives. With this experience, God provided Joel with the kind of leadership development that he would need to exhibit very shortly.

chapter nine

THE LAKEWOOD LEGACY

For I have known him, in order that he may command his children and his household after him, that they keep the way of the LORD, to do righteousness and justice.
—Genesis 18:19

For several years, John and Joel Osteen visited over thirty countries holding crusades and training pastors how to better reach out to those around them. Joel videotaped everything during the trips and, when they returned to Houston, he would edit the tapes for the television ministry.

But for Joel, this was more than videotaping his father's various meetings and crusades. He also experienced his father's heart for ministry. Once, during a quick stop at a remote landing strip, they noticed a young man lying on the ground outside the small terminal. John was drawn to the young man and spent most of an hour with him. When the time came to return to the plane, Joel saw his father reach into his back pocket and give the young man some cash. When they got back on the plane, Joel asked his father, "Daddy, what was that all about? What was that young man doing there? What's his story?"

John replied, "Joel, he was headed back home to the States, but he ran out of money. He's been here for a couple of weeks, all alone, stranded. So I gave him enough money to get home. When I got off the plane and saw him lying there on the ground, I had so much compassion for him. I just wanted to pick him up and hug him. I wanted to love and comfort him, and tell him that he was going to make it. All I could think about was What if that was one of my sons? What if that were you? What if that were Paul? What if that was one of my daughters? And I knew how I would want somebody to help one of my children!"

A few years later, in India, John and Joel were traveling back to the hotel at two o'clock in the morning when their car broke down. They were stranded in the middle of nowhere in a country where they knew no one, and neither of them spoke the language. Within a short period of time, fifty or sixty people had surrounded their vehicle. It was becoming a tense situation since Americans were not commonly seen or welcome in that section of India.

Suddenly, a large luxury car approached out of nowhere. It was unusual for a car to be in that part of India at any time, much less in the middle of the night. The driver spotted John and Joel along the side of the road and, much to their surprise, stopped. A man stepped out, assessed the situation, and spoke to them in English: "Don't be afraid. I'm going to take you where you need to go." Although they had never seen the man before, they got into his car. He drove them the full five hours back to their hotel! When they offered to pay him for his trouble, he refused their money. John and Joel harvested from the seed that John had planted in an airport years before.

From time to time, Joel's wife, Victoria, traveled with them to help out. She cared for John's hair and makeup for television. Joel and Victoria told John that it was their job to make him look good; it was his job to preach.

In every sense of the term, Joel was an apprentice. For centuries, this was the preferred method of training for all kinds of professionals. His training included watching thousands of hours of videotaped sermons and seeing the heart and faith of his father in action as he reached out with arms and hands to touch thousands of people for healing and deliverance all over the world. He was being trained by witnessing, firsthand, the vision of a man who wanted to make a difference in the world. His father knew that if he could lead enough people to Jesus and train them to lead others to Jesus, it would impact the world with the power of God. Working so closely with one of the most successful pastors in America allowed Joel to meet and work with important people around the world. From these engagements, Joel received the confidence that he could work with anybody, regardless of his or her position, and not be intimidated by title or reputation.

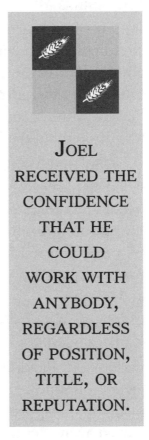

JOEL RECEIVED THE CONFIDENCE THAT HE COULD WORK WITH ANYBODY, REGARDLESS OF POSITION, TITLE, OR REPUTATION.

This vision of impacting the world was being birthed within Victoria as well. She had not been raised in a pastor's home and didn't have the benefit of being exposed to John every day as Joel had over the years. This time with John allowed Victoria to grow in the Lord and learn from him as well. She also witnessed Joel being used in a marvelous way by God.

A FAMILY AFFAIR

Other members of the Osteen family also became involved in the ministry of Lakewood Church. Justin Osteen, John's son from his first marriage, owned and operated a management consultation firm with a nationwide clientele of nonprofit and government organizations before reuniting with his father to serve as the administrator of Lakewood, where he conducted training seminars on church administration for pastors throughout the United States.

John and Dodie's daughter Lisa also joined the Lakewood staff, serving as the Director of Ministries, supervising twenty-five volunteer ministries as well as the publication and literature outreaches of John Osteen Ministries. Eventually, Lisa met and married Kevin Comes at Lakewood. Another daughter, April, and her husband, Gary, worked with music and youth.

Their eldest daughter, Tamara, and her husband, Jim Graff, worked at Lakewood for a time before moving on to a pastorate in Victoria, Texas. During this time, Paul was completing his studies to become a surgeon. By the early eighties, Justin had resigned his position as church administrator and moved away. But this was a special time for John and Dodie, to be working with four of their five children in the church at the same time. Joel remarked to Victoria during this period, "We've got to really enjoy this time. We're not always going to be here together as a family."[39]

During the 1980s, John's health became a concern. By 1986, John was told that he had blockages in his heart. A date was selected for John to have a heart catheterization procedure. During the procedure, emergency bypass surgery was deemed necessary and a quadruple bypass was performed on John's heart to save his life. The surgery was successful, and soon John returned to all of his duties at Lakewood and continued to travel all over the world.

TERROR AT LAKEWOOD

At about eleven o'clock on the morning of January 30, 1990, John's daughter, Lisa Comes, was routinely opening mail in her office when she noticed a brown-papered package addressed to her father. There was nothing unusual about the package. It had been sent from Elizabethtown, North Carolina, and was heavier than most they received. While Lisa was sitting in her office with the package on her lap, a powerful, deafening pipe bomb exploded from within, riddling her office with debris, nails, shrapnel, and barbed wire and setting the office on fire. Lisa ran screaming from the office as other staff members rushed to her assistance. Lisa was first taken to Ben Taub Hospital and then to Methodist Hospital.

John had not gone into the office at the usual time. He had been awakened earlier that morning by the hand of God, gone into the den to get his Bible, and there felt the presence of God. As the morning went by, John attempted to leave his house to go to the church, but he felt held back by a supernatural force. While he was still at home, word reached him about what had happened to Lisa. The force no longer held him back. John drove straight to the hospital.

97

The doctors were able to close three holes in Lisa's abdomen created by the fire of the blast without having to use skin grafts. Miraculously, Lisa's life was spared; not one piece of metal from the bomb had penetrated her body. One of the emergency officials on the scene told John, "Pastor, I want you to know that someone had to be standing between your daughter and that bomb."

Pastors from all over Houston came to pray for Lisa, including John's good friend, John Bisango, pastor of First Baptist Church of Houston. Calls and telegrams flooded in from across the country.

Federal investigators interviewed one suspect who had been arrested in Orange County after police noticed switches, wiring, and other materials in his car that could be used to make a bomb. But he was eventually released. Investigators also routinely questioned Lisa's first husband, but he was immediately eliminated as a suspect since he had been in Hawaii at the time of the bombing.[40]

PEOPLE RESPOND TO JOHN'S MESSAGE

Through the mid-1980s and into the 1990s, Lakewood Church's television ministry reached out to people not only in Houston, but also around the United States. The church was recognized as the eleventh largest church in America in worship attendance and the sixth largest in Sunday school attendance for the years 1983–84.[41] Lakewood was also recognized as among the top fifty churches in the country in conversions and baptisms.[42] Lakewood Church was listed as the seventeenth largest church in America in worship attendance and as the thirteenth fastest-growing church in 1989–1990.[43]

John constantly preached messages of encouragement. He would always encourage young pastors to preach sermons that built their people up, not ones that tore them down. He would encourage them to preach messages of hope for a better future and of how God's love would enable people to have a better life here on earth. John knew how much people needed the Lord to help them in their daily walk through the stresses and struggles of life. In one such message, he taught that people should endeavor to think God's thoughts daily! Renew your mind. Learn to think as God thinks about salvation, forgiveness, mercy, healing, deliverance, love, goodness, and all the other wonderful things in His Word.[44]

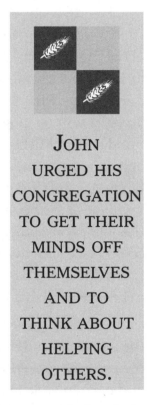

JOHN URGED HIS CONGREGATION TO GET THEIR MINDS OFF THEMSELVES AND TO THINK ABOUT HELPING OTHERS.

John also taught on maturing in our Christian walk. He said, "The spirit of the world exalts self. Gimmee, gimmee, gimmee, and get, get, get. It's a shame when people think only of themselves— the big 'I'—and cease to care about others." John added, "They need to have their 'I' knocked out!"[45]

John would encourage his congregation to get their minds off themselves and to think about helping others. Visit someone who is sick, say hello to that lonely neighbor down the street, and thank God daily for family and friends. Drop an extra check in the offering at church in support of someone on the mission field. John stressed that success wasn't measured in what you accumulate for yourself—it's what you do for others that counts with God.

John taught that hope was very important. Without hope, faith alone doesn't produce results. John and Dodie always mixed lots of faith with lots of hope. If John got discouraged about something, Dodie would make sure that he practiced what he preached.

The diversity of the church had a wide appeal that translated into a diverse television audience as well. John had a saying about the Bible that he would lead the congregation in reciting just before each message: "This is my Bible. I am what it says I am. I have what it says I have. I can do what it says I can do. Today, I will be taught the Word of God. I boldly confess. My mind is alert. My heart is receptive. I will never be the same. I am about to receive the incorruptible, indestructible, ever living seed of the Word of God. I will never be the same. Never, never, never. I will never be the same. In Jesus' name. Amen." This reassured the television audience as well as the congregation that they could place faith in the Word of God, that John's messages were grounded in the Bible, and that from them they could learn how to believe in all that God has in store for those who love Him.

John always looked straight into the camera and welcomed the television audience to join in the service. At the end of each message, he looked into the camera and invited the television audience to welcome Jesus into their hearts and accept Jesus as Savior. Prior to ending the broadcast John would recite another saying that proved to be prophetic:

> Great it is to dream the dream
> And stand in life by the starry stream.
> But the greater thing
> Is to fight life through
> And say at the end,
> "The dream is true!"

Throughout the last part of the 1990s, Joel encouraged his father to boldly reach out and expand the ministry. He also encouraged him to expand the television ministry and reach out to the major cities in the United States through additional cable networks—allowing Lakewood to touch millions of additional homes. He encouraged John to syndicate the program to individual stations in major cities across the United States. Joel wanted his father to contact media outlets and do what could be done to add the program to cable and satellite networks around the world. He wanted John to conduct services in large auditoriums and arenas in major cities across the country. Joel envisioned Lakewood touching millions of lives. He also encouraged his dad to start several new programs at the Lakewood Church location in order to reach new highs in weekly attendance and the involvement of local members.

John responded by reminding Joel that he was now seventy-five years old and just wanted to maintain his schedule at the church and continue the television ministry as it was. John told Joel that he did not think that this was the time. Little did they know that God was preparing Joel for the days ahead. God was planting a vision in Joel's heart for what He had in store for Lakewood Church. Joel respected the authority of his father, not only as his father but as pastor of Lakewood Church and as the leader of the ministry. He did not argue with his father's decision. But he kept all those things in his heart that the Lord had given him.

chapter ten

THE END OF
AN ERA

His mercy endures forever.
—Psalm 106:1

To everything there is a season, a time for every
purpose under heaven.
—Ecclesiastes 3:1

Whether it was just God's timing or the impact of being on national television, Lakewood Church grew extensively. By the end of the 1990s, Lakewood Church was recognized as one of the ten largest churches in America. But John's health battles were a continuing problem. John had been suffering from kidney trouble because of lifelong high blood pressure. He was on dialysis until a kidney could be found for a transplant. Still, he managed to maintain his work schedule.

But on Monday night, January 11, 1999, a sickly John called Joel's home to ask if he would preach that coming Sunday. Joel told his father no.

John said, "Joel, you're my first choice."

But Joel still said that he couldn't do it, hung up the phone, and sat down to eat his dinner.

"I had never preached before," recalled Joel. "It was kind of a weird thing. I never wanted to preach, but I knew in my heart that it was what I was supposed to do. I knew I was supposed to step up."

To this day, Joel isn't entirely sure why he was his father's first choice that night. After all, John could have picked from any of his children or their spouses; all of them were involved in the ministry. But his father's insistence stuck in Joel's head, and as he was sitting there eating his dinner, something came over him. He felt like he had received a message, like God was saying he should go for it. So he called his father back and agreed to preach for the first time. Then, Joel spent the rest of the week thinking he'd made the biggest mistake of his life.

By the time Sunday rolled around, John was in the hospital, although doctors reassured the family it was nothing serious. Not wanting John to miss his youngest son delivering a sermon for the first time, the Osteens hooked up a phone line from the hospital to the church. Just before the service, Joel's mouth dried up, and his lips refused to separate from his teeth. He was extremely nervous about filling the pulpit of his famous and beloved father. Seeking comfort and reassurance, Joel slipped on a pair of his father's shoes and wore them on his big day.

Once on stage, Joel tore through his sermon at a nervous, breakneck pace. "You know, I just told stories about our family. I made them laugh," he remembers. "The Lord just helped me get through my message, and I could speak." But deep down, Joel said to himself, *Man, I'll never get a shot at another message.*

John listened to the service through the telephone connection at the hospital. He was very proud of his son. A nurse later told Joel how proud his dad was to hear him preach. Joel was somewhat glad that he would never have to do it again. Unfortunately, it was the last sermon John would ever hear.

John was not well, but was released from the hospital and went home, where he continued to undergo dialysis. On Friday night, John called his son-in-law Gary and asked him to come sit with him. Dodie was tired and John knew she needed some rest.

Early on Saturday morning, January 23, 1999, John momentarily woke from his sleep and uttered his final words, "God's mercy endures forever." Minutes later, he suffered a major heart attack. The paramedics were immediately called and were able to resuscitate him. He was taken to St Luke's Episcopal Hospital. John Osteen passed away that afternoon.

MOURNING THEIR LEADER

On Sunday morning, January 24, Dodie, her children, their spouses, and her grandchildren walked on stage at Lakewood to tell the assembled congregation that John was gone. The congregation wept openly. For many, John had been the only pastor they had ever known. Dodie assured the congregation that the work that John had started would carry on. Joel told the press that he, his mother, and his two sisters would carry on his dad's work, sharing the Sunday morning services between them. "It will continue to be our family. I don't think it will be any one individual."[46] John's funeral service was announced for the following Wednesday at Lakewood.

The funeral was to be a celebration of John's life. The city of Houston joined in mourning with the Lakewood Church family as well as the Osteen family. City Council meetings normally held on Wednesdays were cancelled to allow those who wished to go to the funeral. Many friends from the charismatic and evangelical world came to celebrate his life. Political figures from both Washington and Texas came together to mourn his passing. Missionaries from several countries flew into Houston for the service. When the time came, the auditorium was filled to capacity.

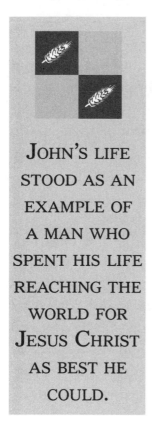

JOHN'S LIFE STOOD AS AN EXAMPLE OF A MAN WHO SPENT HIS LIFE REACHING THE WORLD FOR JESUS CHRIST AS BEST HE COULD.

Bravely, the family took to the stage as Dodie conducted the service for her beloved husband. Many people were given the opportunity to speak and share their special memories of John. Mayor Lee Brown spoke and said that John was "the tree that bore much fruit in the word of God." Good friends of John who represented the breadth and depth of the charismatic movement spoke and shared their thoughts, including R. W. Schambach; Richard Roberts, on behalf of his father Oral Roberts; Kenneth Copeland; T. L. Osborn; and Kenneth Hagin Jr., on behalf of his father, Kenneth Hagin Sr. They spoke of John's integrity and called him a pastor of pastors. The sanctuary was filled with people who had their own memories of their pastor. These were not well-known names in the Christian world, but merely people whom John had cared for, prayed for, and reached for Jesus.

At the end of the service, John's coffin was brought into the sanctuary. The pallbearers carried their beloved pastor around the front of the stage while a bagpipe played "Amazing Grace." Following the public service, John was buried in Klein Memorial Park, in Tomball, Texas. The burial was a private affair attended only by members of the immediate family. John's life was a tribute to a man who spent his life reaching the world for Jesus Christ as best he could.

CARRYING ON

Dodie and the entire Osteen family always thought that John would eventually overcome his health problems and return to the task for which God had called him. But now Lakewood Church was without a senior pastor for the first time in its history.

After John's death, two things were immediately apparent: first, no one was certain who would fill the shoes of John Osteen; and second, John's death would not be the death of Lakewood Church. While he was alive, whenever John was asked about his future successor at Lakewood, all he would say was that God would provide the right person for the task when the time came. At the funeral, Mayor Brown assured the congregation that he was certain that the work of Lakewood Church would continue. But no one knew if the mayor was speaking from fact or from the hope of everyone's heart. Dodie continued to tell everyone of the family's commitment to continue the work of her late husband.

On Monday morning, three days after the death of his father, Joel was at home contemplating all the events that had taken place. He had been working for his father for seventeen years now. John Osteen had been pastor of Lakewood for Joel's entire life. Joel did what his earthly father had taught him to do in times of crisis and uncertainty—go to God in prayer. As he did, he felt an overwhelming desire to speak at Lakewood again. Joel called his mother and said, "Mother, who's going to speak on Sunday?"

She said, "Well, Joel, I don't know. We're going to have to pray and believe that God will send the right one."

Joel said, "Well, I'm just sort of thinking about...maybe that I would like to do it."

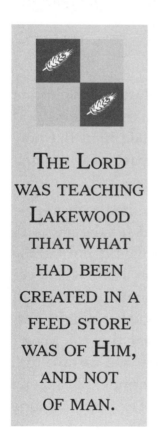

THE LORD WAS TEACHING LAKEWOOD THAT WHAT HAD BEEN CREATED IN A FEED STORE WAS OF HIM, AND NOT OF MAN.

Dodie Osteen has an interesting habit. When she is on the telephone and is finished with the conversation, she's through. She just hangs up, giving the other party no time to respond. This occasion was no different; Dodie had heard all she needed to hear. She told him, "Oh, Joel, that would be great. I can't wait to tell the people. We'll see you later." Click. The line was dead.

Joel replied to no one, "Now, wait a minute. I said I was thinking about speaking. I didn't say I was going to do it."

Too late. She was gone.

Two days later, at the memorial service, and in front of eight thousand people, Dodie announced that Joel would be speaking the following Sunday. Joel was locked in.

Many people were concerned about the future of Lakewood Church. The family may have been certain that the church would go on, but no one knew exactly how that would happen. John had always said that he would preach until he was in his nineties, but that was not to be. The local media openly discussed the future of Lakewood Church without its founder. Many speculated that Lakewood had little chance of surviving. The naysayers were quick to point out that no large church with a strong, dynamic presence like John Osteen had ever survived the death of its leader.

The church membership was not certain what would happen either. Many were concerned that Lakewood would never be the same again. Some urged the church to cut back on expenses as much as possible, anticipating a drop in giving and smaller attendance. But God was doing a work in the midst of His people's sorrow. This was a time for the Lord to teach the Lakewood family that what had been created in a feed store nearly forty years before was of Him, and not of man.

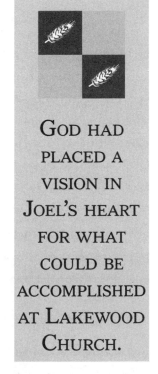

GOD HAD PLACED A VISION IN JOEL'S HEART FOR WHAT COULD BE ACCOMPLISHED AT LAKEWOOD CHURCH.

As much as Joel tried to make light of the reports, the words still stung. There he was, trying to get up his nerve to speak, trying to build his confidence, and the media and critics were predicting the demise of Lakewood Church. The naysayers predicted that Lakewood Church would do well if they could merely maintain the status quo in the months and years to come.

God allowed Saul to reign for forty years. But long before the death of Saul, He had been preparing David to lead Israel. Being a shepherd was not the typical training for a future king, but God had been building David's faith and creating a relationship between them. He learned to trust in God without question. David also reigned for forty years, and during that time God prepared Solomon for leadership. Under Solomon's leadership Israel prospered as never before. Solomon did not become what he could have been because he fell away from his trust in God.

Whether it was a coincidence that, like these men, John led Lakewood for nearly forty years, only God in His infinite wisdom knows. But, the truth is that God had been preparing someone for the task for seventeen years. God had placed a vision in the heart of Joel for what could be accomplished at Lakewood Church. Joel had talked to his dad about it, but the time had not been right. He had been given a vision for Lakewood Church, not for what God wanted John to do, but for what He wanted Joel to do when the time came.

God had a plan in place. Everything was happening in the proper time. With the death of John, the time had come for the events to unfold as God had planned.

A LEADER EMERGES

Joel decided not to dwell on public opinion or popularity polls. He refused to let those negative reports poison his heart and mind. He declined to listen to anyone who seemed intent on talking him out of fulfilling his destiny. More important, he knew that God had raised up Lakewood Church to be a beacon of hope for more than forty years, and he wasn't going to let it go down the drain just because his dad had gone to heaven. He also had faith in the calling of God in his life. Besides, Joel would not be the first person to have his calling questioned:

> And when He had come to His own country, He taught them in their synagogue, so that they were astonished and said, "Where did this Man get this wisdom and these mighty works? Is this not the carpenter's son? Is not His mother called Mary? And His brothers James, Joses, Simon, and Judas? And His sisters, are they not all with us? Where then did this Man get all these things?" So they were offended at Him. But Jesus said to them, "A prophet is not without honor except in his own country and in his own house."
>
> (Matthew 13:54–57)

Jesus knew that He had to be obedient to His Father. Joel also knew that he had to be obedient to the calling God had on his life. Regardless of the negative things that were being reported by the press and the concerns of many well-meaning people, God's plan had to come to pass.

In the next thirty-six weeks, Joel spoke on thirty-three Sunday mornings. The other members of the Osteen family continued to do the work of the Lord at Lakewood. But they began to see the hand of the Lord at work in the situation.

The very first Sunday after John's funeral, the Lord spoke to Lisa, "I always sat behind my dad to assist him. So when Joel was sitting there and getting ready to preach—he was so nervous—I was sitting behind him, and I leaned up to say something to him, and in that split second the Lord spoke to me down in my spirit, and He said, 'Lisa, I am transitioning you to work with your brother, and just as you served your dad, I want you to serve your brother as pastor of this church.'

I knew that was the Lord who had said that to me, and I was so happy after that."[47]

Dodie also explained how she learned of Joel's calling to lead the church. "Not long after John had died, Joel said, 'Mama, I need to talk to you. I think God is calling me to be the pastor of this church.' I said, 'What?!' I thought, *He was the last one I'd expect.* He didn't want to get up there and be the pastor, but he felt like it was God's will."

This time of transition brought an overall stability to the church and calmed the nerves of many of those who were concerned. The church missed the leadership and vision that John had provided, but the fears that the church would disintegrate passed. There were still those who had questions and others who were waiting for the church to fail, but God had other plans.

Joel knew that he was not his father, but he wasn't supposed to be. He began to see God's hand in all that was happening. This is certainly not to suggest that God caused John Osteen's death, but that there is a timing of God that is determined before the beginning of time. In His foreknowledge, God knows things that are to be before they become.

It is a familiar pattern seen throughout Scripture. There was a time for Moses to lead the people of Israel, but there came a time for Joshua to succeed him. Moses was called the greatest prophet who ever lived in the history of Israel, but it was Joshua who led the people into the Promised Land. Joshua had served as an assistant to Moses for many years. He had been there to see the parting of the Red Sea and the manna from heaven, and he had stood at the entrance to the Tent of Meeting when Moses would meet with God concerning the future of the children of Israel. But it was Joshua who would lead the Israelites in the defeat of their enemies and in the possession of the land that God had given them.

John Osteen had taken Lakewood Church to a place that few pastors in the United States have ever experienced. Little did he know, little did anyone know, that all he had done was bring them to the edge of the Promised Land. He had given them a glimpse of what was to come.

Again, God had birthed a vision and a desire in the heart of Joel during an earlier time. But it wasn't the right time. Now the time had come for a new generation to take the role of leaders at Lakewood Church. Joel believed that God was preparing a new generation for a new century. A new century that would bring things to pass that could only be imagined.

Lakewood Church began to accept Joel's leadership. They had accepted the death of their founding pastor. Although John was still missed and thought of with love and affection, they were comforted by the reality that the church would go on and the Lord's work would continue. It had been assumed that, after the death of John, Lakewood would wait a year to name a new senior pastor. But as time went on, it became apparent that God's calling was upon Joel. The church needed direction and vision. Vision Sunday was scheduled for October 3, 1999, when Joel would officially be named as senior pastor of Lakewood.

Joel had to prepare himself for the task to which God had called him. All kinds of negative thoughts bombarded his mind. The critics talked about how Lakewood was never going to make it, that they would surely go under. Joel heard all these negative reports. He had to decide if he was going to follow the direction the Lord had laid before him or if he was going to believe the critics. When he got up in the morning he would hear or read the negative reports. He had to decide that he would not dwell on these things. He would say to himself, "I am well able to do what God has called me to do."

Some Sundays, when he got to the pulpit, he was so nervous he would need to hold on to the podium. But he would say to himself, "Joel, you are strong in the Lord and in the power of His might. You are anointed. Greater is He that is in you than he that is in the world." He was allowing God to change him from a man who worked behind the scenes, never seen or heard in public, to a man God could use to change a city and impact the world for Jesus Christ. Joel knew he was more prepared for this task than people were aware.

chapter eleven

A VISION FOR
THE FUTURE

And it shall come to pass afterward that I will pour out My Spirit
on all flesh; your sons and your daughters shall prophesy, your old
men shall dream dreams, your young men shall see visions.
—Joel 2:28

O n October 3, 1999, Joel Osteen assumed the title and
responsibility of senior pastor of Lakewood Church.
Joel had shared with his family his sense of God's
calling to assume the responsibility and step into his father's
shoes. There was no formal vote by a board or committee, but
a consensus was felt. Also, since he had preached over 90 percent of the time since his father's death, the church was getting comfortable with the idea of Joel as pastor.

On that same day, the *Houston Chronicle* printed an interview with Joel. It disclosed that Joel had been ordained since
1992. But local scholars were quoted as saying it would be
difficult for Lakewood to thrive under Joel's leadership. One
scholar referred to Franklin Graham assuming the leadership
of the Billy Graham Evangelistic Association. He added that it
was especially difficult when there was a television ministry
involved, such as Richard Roberts replacing his father Oral Roberts as president of Oral Roberts University. The article ended

by saying that when the founder dies, often the ministry dies as well.[48]

These had to be difficult words for Joel to read in his hometown newspaper. But Joel knew his father well, and he knew more than anyone how difficult it was for anyone to replace him. John had started Lakewood in 1959; Joel wasn't born until 1962. Joel had never known any other church. He loved Lakewood. The people of Lakewood were his family in every way. Joel knew that God had called him to this task, but he also knew that he didn't want to let anybody down.

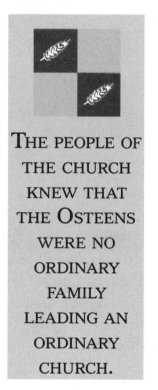

THE PEOPLE OF THE CHURCH KNEW THAT THE OSTEENS WERE NO ORDINARY FAMILY LEADING AN ORDINARY CHURCH.

But Joel was much more than just a young man assuming leadership of a megachurch. Joel had the strong support of his family. Dodie was still cofounder and a direct link to the past glories of Lakewood Church. She had witnessed the miracles; she had been present when God provided the cash to build the buildings. Dodie was the Baptist preacher's wife who had not only experienced her own healing, but had also seen her little girl healed.

The other members of the Osteen family had their own stories to tell. Lisa had survived a bomb exploding in her lap. Paul had been healed of malaria when traveling with his father on a mission trip. All these testimonies to God's power and faithfulness added up to a great deal of credibility as a leadership team. The people of the church knew that this was no ordinary family leading an ordinary church. This was a family with a sacred trust left to them by God and their patriarch, about which they would be extremely careful.

VISION SUNDAY

Joel's first Sunday as senior pastor, Vision Sunday, was a great service designed to inspire and encourage everyone. Joel opened the service with all his usual nervous excitement; it was obvious that he felt that this was the will and plan of God. But he also knew there would still be those who were less than convinced. As the morning began, Joel spoke of Joseph and how, as a young man, the Lord had given Joseph dreams. These dreams were of himself, the youngest son of Jacob, being in a position of leadership over his brothers. He spoke of how God would be bringing Lakewood through this time of transition. He reassured the people that God had always had His hand on Lakewood and that He would never take it off.

There was special music by Dove and Grammy award winner Bob Carlisle. There were video presentations honoring the life and ministry of John Osteen. There were video testimonies by missionaries about the marvelous work of John and Lakewood Church in touching the world for Jesus Christ. Other members of the Osteen family paid their respects to the past leadership of John one more time, before the focus was turned to the future.

Dodie officially announced that Joel was assuming the position of senior pastor of Lakewood Church. In his first official remarks, he thanked the family for their support. Joel reassured everyone that this was something he was called to do, not something he was doing out of family obligation. Joel reassured everyone that Lakewood would continue to be the church it had always been, with a renewed interest in meeting the needs of the local congregation. He announced that a new and much-needed youth building would soon be constructed. Joel mentioned new ministries that would touch the lives in the community around Lakewood, such as a medical ministry that his brother Paul would be leading. He talked about other goals and plans for the church, including his belief that there would soon be a need for two Sunday services at Lakewood because of the crowds that would be attracted. Some may have thought this to be ambitious, but it proved to be prophetic: within twelve months there would be three services, and in two years, five services!

Then, for the first time, Victoria was introduced to the congregation as the first lady of Lakewood. Victoria also had large shoes to fill. Lakewood had a history of the pastor's wife playing a major role in the services. This was the end of one era and the beginning of a new one. Yet it was also reassuring that Victoria had been around for many years, working with John and traveling with John and Joel overseas.

As Joel ended his message, he announced that a number of special speakers would be coming to Lakewood over the next year. Some interpreted this as Joel saying, *If you don't think my preaching is good enough for you to stay, you will still get to hear some of the best speakers in the charismatic movement.*

This first service was important in two ways: first, Joel immediately began to institute changes that would transform Lakewood from one of America's many megachurches to the largest church in America; and second, the service signified a passing of the torch to a new generation of leadership at Lakewood Church. They had closed the chapter on the ministry of John Osteen and opened the book on the ministry of Joel Osteen.

But few could have imagined what God had in store for Lakewood over the next few years; even the next few months would be amazing.

The Reverend John Osteen, pastor of Lakewood Church, November 1981.
Reprinted by permission of the *Houston Chronicle*.

A familiar sight: John Osteen preaching before the TV cameras in 1987. Reprinted by permission of the *Houston Chronicle*.

Joel Osteen, on screen, during the congregation's ground-breaking service at the Compaq Center in December 2003. Reprinted by permission of the *Houston Chronicle*.

Joel Osteen and his wife, Victoria, welcome the overflow crowd to the opening services of Lakewood Church at the converted Compaq Center on Saturday, July 16, 2005. Reprinted by permission of the *Houston Chronicle*.

Part III

THE MINISTRY OF
JOEL OSTEEN,
LAKEWOOD'S BLESSING

chapter twelve

JOEL'S LEADERSHIP BUILDS A TEAM

Follow Me, and I will make you fishers of men.
—Matthew 4:19

W hen Joel first became senior pastor of Lakewood Church, he said that he was going to make as few changes as he could. There is little doubt that he was sincere. There had certainly been a need to reassure the congregation and to build their confidence in the Osteen family during this time of transition.

Most people tend to see things as they are and only desire to improve on what they have. One thing that separates true leaders and visionaries from other people is the ability to see things not for what they are, but for what they could be. As Joel Osteen became pastor of one of the largest churches in America, he could have maintained the status quo. For many people, simply maintaining a megachurch after the death of its founder would have been hard enough. But Joel did not want to simply maintain; he wanted to take Lakewood toward a level that only he could see at that time. It would be a level that no church in America had ever obtained. And to do so, Joel would need to demonstrate the qualities of a great leader.

VISION

A leader believes in what can be, when no one else around him can see it. A leader understands that he must be the first to see what is to be, and then he must lead everyone toward that vision. This is the very essence of leadership. If everyone else can see what is to be, they will not only follow, but they will also race ahead. Simply organizing people to achieve a corporate goal is not leadership; that's management. Managers can be hired, but leaders are hard to come by.

Joel has demonstrated visionary leadership at every point since he has taken the position of senior pastor of Lakewood Church. He has a vision for what Lakewood Church can be and has made every decision, every hiring, and every communication with the goal of moving toward that vision. This vision is the single leadership trait that sets Joel Osteen apart from thousands of pastors in America and the world. It is the trait that has taken Joel and Lakewood to a level that no other congregation has achieved. Joel Osteen has a vision for what and where he wants to go, and he is taking thousands, if not millions, of people with him. The simplest definition of leadership is this: when you look behind you, is anyone following? Joel Osteen is a leader. The proof is in the millions of people who follow him.

RISK TAKING

A leader understands that you don't achieve what you envision without taking risks. Joel's biggest risk was his willingness to accept the job of senior pastor. When John died and no one knew what was going to happen, Joel stepped up and said, "Follow me." It was a risk for him. He was not expected to take the job. This was not a risk he had to take. There were

126

several candidates for senior pastor on staff at Lakewood. There were other candidates within the family. Lakewood could have undertaken a national search for a senior pastor, and many would have applied for the job. Joel stepped up to the job. When a team is in trouble, most players say, "What are we going to do?" A leader says, "Give me the ball, and everybody follow me."

An additional risk was the expansion of the television ministry. Joel was an inexperienced speaker assuming the role of nationally known television evangelist. Not many people like to fail in private, let alone fail on national TV. Joel stepped up to a national stage and took the risk of potential failure with the whole world watching. A leader knows that if you play it safe all the time, you will never go higher than you are today. Joel refused to play it safe. He accepted the reality that to move to the next level, he would have to take risks.

A LEADER KNOWS THAT IF YOU PLAY IT SAFE ALL THE TIME, YOU WILL NEVER GO HIGHER THAN YOU ARE TODAY.

Joel continues to take risks as the ministry progresses. It was a risk to rent large sporting arenas thousands of miles from Houston and expect to fill them. It was a huge risk to raise money and borrow more in order to renovate a basketball arena into the largest church sanctuary in America. Joel is taking risks each and every day because he is walking a path where no one has ever walked before. When you go into unknown and uncharted territory, the risks are the greatest, but the potential for reward is also the greatest.

TEAMWORK

A single word describes Joel Osteen's approach to leadership: *teamwork*. Taking Lakewood Church to that next level would require more than just what Joel could do; it would take a team. Undoubtedly, Joel has been influenced by many of the great people that he met while working with his dad. One of those people was John Maxwell, former Wesleyan pastor and nationally recognized expert on leadership. One of Maxwell's principles has become a cornerstone of Joel Osteen's leadership style: "one is too small a number to achieve greatness."[49] Joel immediately stepped forward to build the team that could take Lakewood to that next level. Joel had a plan in his mind of where Lakewood Church could go and what steps were required to get there. In that plan were empty spots that had to be filled in order for the plan to be accomplished. Joel was quickly moving ahead to fill the spots.

But it wasn't just a matter of filling spots. Joel wanted the right people, because the plan he envisioned required not just someone, but the right ones. A leader realizes that you don't hire people; you build a team. A team is made up of the right parts, the parts necessary to move an organization forward. There are many who have resumés and exceptional talent, but not everyone is the right person who brings exactly what is needed to the team at just the right time.

DUNCAN DODDS

Among the first additions Joel made to the team at Lakewood was Duncan Dodds as executive director of Lakewood Church and Joel Osteen Ministries. Within a month of Joel's becoming pastor, Duncan came on staff. He was an ordained Southern Baptist minister and formerly served as executive director of Broadcasting Ministries for Second Baptist Church in Houston with Pastor Ed Young. Between the time he worked for Pastor Young and his hiring at Lakewood, he had become the founder and president of a successful consulting company that worked with both large nonprofit organizations and secular corporations across America.

To most people, Lakewood was already at the highest level, but not to Joel. Joel understood another leadership principle from John Maxwell: "a leader's potential is determined by those closest to him."[50] Duncan Dodds was not just a good Christian businessman; he was a man with the knowledge and experience to take the television ministry of Lakewood to the next level. Joel was not satisfied with merely broadcasting on Christian networks and local stations. He wanted the television ministry of Lakewood to be the best in evangelical Christianity. He wanted to reach people whom no one had ever reached, people who had no idea that they were lost. There was a spot on the team for someone who knew how to make that happen. Of course, Duncan Dodds didn't need a job; he wasn't unemployed. But part of leadership is knowing who you want, and going after them.

Today, Duncan is responsible for taking the message and vision of Joel Osteen beyond the walls of the local church through television, publishing, music, special events, ministry resources, and the Internet. He coordinates media buying and handles the negotiation of contracts with television networks and individual stations. This position has taken on even more importance as the ministry has taken to the road. There are a great many details to be considered in organizing the various events at arenas and stadiums across America. Many people work long hours with Duncan to ensure that Joel, Victoria, and the worship team can minister to thousands of people for a couple of hours each week.

There are few individuals with the experience and talents of Duncan Dodds. Duncan's acceptance of the position, working for a young man who had been preaching for less than a year, showed that he was following the direction of God. When Duncan Dodds came on staff neither he nor Joel knew what God had in store for them and the ministry of Lakewood Church in the next few years.

Don Iloff

Another person whom Joel brought onto the administrative team of Lakewood was a family member, Victoria's brother Don Iloff. Don worked in the White House during the administration of President George H. W. Bush. Today, he is the president and general manager of KTBU-TV, channel 55. Don also provides expertise in media relations for Joel on a volunteer basis. Although he has been deeply involved in politics in the past, Don understands that for Joel to become involved in political debates could greatly limit his ability to plant the seed of God's message in the hearts of people. Politics in today's world can be very polarizing, and this is not the goal of Joel and the ministry of Lakewood. With other members of the media team, he helps Joel to determine if everything is being done for Lakewood to touch Houston, the United States, and the world for Jesus Christ.

Cindy Cruse-Ratliff

Among the first challenges Joel faced was the ministry of praise and worship. April and Gary Simon, Joel's sister and brother-in-law, had led praise and worship and worked with the youth during the last few years of John's ministry. But they had left Lakewood to plant High Point Church in Arlington, Texas. Joel knew that praise and worship would greatly define the worship environment at Lakewood. After the pastor, the praise and worship leaders are perhaps the most visible positions in a church. He was also striving to develop a standard of excellence in every area at Lakewood. He needed someone who could carry that standard into praise and worship.

Cindy Cruse-Ratliff had a strong background in Christian music. Her family, The Cruse Family Singers, toured the country and the world singing contemporary Christian music from 1971 to 1985. Cindy's father, Joe Cruse Jr., had been a Southern Baptist pastor. Their music ministry released twenty-five albums and they received two Dove awards in 1978 for their album *Transformation*. Cindy became the youngest ASCAP-licensed songwriter at the age of nine and has written and produced over one hundred recordings. She has also received Dove Awards for Album of the Year and a nomination for Songwriter of the Year. In late 1999, Cindy was leading praise and worship at Covenant Church, a multicultural congregation in the Dallas area. This was where she met her husband Marcus Ratliff.

Cindy received a call one day from a friend telling her that Joel Osteen was going to call her. Cindy was familiar with the situation at Lakewood because her father had been keeping up with the church since Pastor John had passed away. Cindy was aware that many people were watching Joel to see what would happen with the church. A few days later Joel did call, just weeks after he had assumed his position as senior pastor. Cindy was impressed that Joel took the time to deal with this situation personally. At first, she and Marcus did not feel led to move to Houston, but every time they visited Lakewood their hearts turned more and more. Joel remained very persistent. He knew that God was going to do something special at Lakewood and that he desperately wanted Cindy and her husband to be a part of it. After a short time, they fell in love with the people of Lakewood. The music department was very small, but had great potential. By January 2000, just three months after Joel became pastor, Cindy accepted the position of praise and worship leader of Lakewood Church.[51]

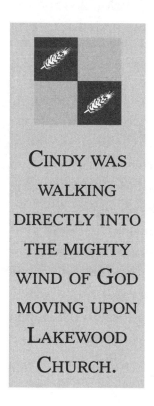

CINDY WAS WALKING DIRECTLY INTO THE MIGHTY WIND OF GOD MOVING UPON LAKEWOOD CHURCH.

Cindy could not have known that she was walking into the mighty wind of God moving upon Lakewood. Almost immediately after she joined the staff, a second service was added to handle the growing crowds. For twelve years Lakewood had been in the same auditorium with one Sunday morning service. By September 2000, it was necessary to add a third service on Saturday evening. In eleven months, Lakewood had gone from one service to three, and weekly attendance had exploded from about six thousand to nearly twenty thousand. The church was bursting with growth, and it was all the staff could do to keep up. With the rapid growth of the church and the expansion into additional services, by the summer of 2000, Cindy was leading worship at every service, and it was overloading her. For her to be her best, Cindy needed some help, and so she called a friend.[52]

ISRAEL HOUGHTON

Israel Houghton's life growing up was almost the opposite of Joel Osteen's and Cindy Cruse-Ratliff's. Israel's mother was an unwed white girl, pregnant by her black boyfriend, in the small town of Waterloo, Iowa. Her parents advised her to abort the baby and get on with her life, or she would no longer be welcome in their home. Israel's mother was an accomplished concert pianist; she had everything going for her. A baby did not fit the plan for her life. But she refused to get the abortion, causing her to be shunned by her family almost completely for the rest of her life. By the time she was eight months pregnant, her boyfriend had left and she was in San Diego, California, addicted to drugs and all alone. The state of California was threatening to take her baby away when it was born. She was standing on the corner of Carlsbad Avenue when a Hispanic lady stopped and said to her, "I don't know you, and I don't want to give you a hard time, but I was driving by and I really felt the need to come tell you that Jesus loves you. You're not forgotten. You did the right thing. It's going to be all right." At that moment, she got on her knees and gave her life to Jesus Christ. The Hispanic woman gave her a place to live until she gave birth to Israel and was able to create a life for the both of them.[53]

She was given a Bible when her son was born and she decided to name him something that she found on nearly every page: Israel. Israel grew up attending a Hispanic church until he was eighteen. He is a walking illustration of the diversity of Lakewood Church: an African-American man with a white mother who grew up in a Hispanic church. At nineteen, while serving as drummer at a church in Phoenix, Arizona, he was asked to lead praise and worship. At that time he only knew three songs written by Ron Kenoly, and so he led the people in them week after week. Finally, a lady came up to him and said, "You might want to go find your sound, and go find who you are." Israel knew he was born to worship. He knew this was what he was created for. Worship became his lifestyle.[54]

Eventually, Israel met Fred Hammond and became a part of his group, Radical for Christ, where he worked with many of the most prominent voices in gospel music, including CeCe Winans, Donnie McClurkin, Andrae Crouch, and Gary Oliver. Later, Israel started his own group, New Breed, made up of several praise and worship leaders from across America. Israel has also worked with the Young Messiah Tour and Promise Keepers.

Cindy's call brought Israel to Lakewood, where they lead praise and worship, as well as write new praise and worship songs.

DAKRI BROWN

Israel soon introduced a young man to Cindy, Dakri Brown. Dakri is a young African-American man and a member of New Breed who is now the vocal music director at Lakewood. Dakri directs the choir, as well as the small ensemble groups. He brings great enthusiasm to the task combined with a humble, giving, loving, and serving spirit. It is easy to see that the choir responds to Dakri. They want to sing for him. They respond to his commands and direction. Since the church moved to the Compaq Center, the choir has grown to over five hundred members, not counting the Spanish choir. Some observers have noted that the Lakewood choir is fast becoming known as one of the great choirs in America, along with such groups as the Brooklyn Tabernacle Choir and the Mormon Tabernacle Choir.

Together, Cindy Cruse-Ratliff, Israel Houghton, and Dakri Brown form one of the strongest collections of musical talent found at any local church in the United States. The Lakewood music department has released two CDs. Both have gone platinum and received critical acclaim in the United States and around the world.

MARCOS WITT

For Lakewood Church, reaching out into the community has always included the Hispanic community. Again, even before John's passing, sermons were simultaneously translated into Spanish each week through the use of low-power FM signals. Many of John's books and tapes were also translated into Spanish. But to place an even greater focus on Spanish ministry, Joel went looking for someone who had the credentials and anointing to build one of the largest Hispanic ministries in the United States. Joel found that man in Marcos Witt.

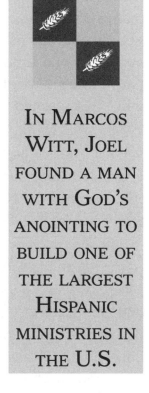

IN MARCOS WITT, JOEL FOUND A MAN WITH GOD'S ANOINTING TO BUILD ONE OF THE LARGEST HISPANIC MINISTRIES IN THE U.S.

Marcos was born in San Antonio, Texas, in 1962. When he was a month old, his parents moved to Durango, Mexico, where they served as missionaries. Marcos was the second of three sons. In 1964, his father died while dropping gospel leaflets from a plane into a remote Mexican village high in the mountains. Something happened to the plane's engine, and it crashed, immediately killing Jerry Witt and his fellow missionary. Their bodies were pulled from the plane and taken to the county seat where local villagers jeered and spit on them for daring to bring the gospel to their area. Another missionary bribed officials for the return of the bodies so they could be buried. Alone, Marcos' mother continued the missionary work after his father's death.[55]

Three years later, Marcos's mother met Frank Warren, a man who was searching for God's plan for his life. God gave him the plan by making him a husband, father, and missionary, all at one time. At a young age, Marcos would accompany his stepfather to the towns and villages around Durango while he preached the gospel.

Marcos studied classical music for ten years in different venues. He studied at the State University of Durango (Universidad de Juarez de Durango), by extension courses through the University of Nebraska, and at a private conservatory in San Antonio. In 1986, Marcos married his wife, Miriam.

In 2002, Marcos and Miriam accepted the position of Hispanic pastors at Lakewood. At present, the Hispanic service meets on Sunday afternoons, immediately following the second Sunday morning English service. Lakewood does not have a Hispanic congregation; it has a Spanish service. It is all Lakewood. It is a complete Spanish Lakewood service with a choir and band. English interpretation is available in this service. This service is also recorded and broadcast over stations in Houston as well as cable networks throughout the United States and Latin America. Joel said his goal was to help the rapidly growing population of Hispanics in the Houston area. Lakewood's move downtown to the Compaq Center has been a positive thing for the Hispanic community; there is greater access by public transportation than there was when the church was in East Houston.

Speaking about the commitment that Joel and Lakewood were making to the Hispanic community, Marcos Witt said, "The deal with Joel is that he really understands that to reach Hispanics correctly there really had to be a cultural context."[56] At present, the service ministers to about seven thousand people each week. The Hispanic outreach mirrors the ministries offered in the English-speaking congregation, with small groups, retreat weekends, leadership training, and social services available.

Marcos's experience in Latin America has served him well. Though many in the congregation have roots in Mexico, the crowd is international, with members from countries including Colombia, El Salvador, Honduras, and Argentina. In his sermons, Marcos makes references to soccer or to stars from Telemundo television programs. The services have a distinctive Latin flavor that resonates with his audience in a way that could only be created by Hispanic pastor. But Marcos maintains the positive message as much as Joel does. He agrees philosophically that it is the task of the church to lift people up, not tear them down. He emphasizes that God loves us and it is up to us to accept His love. This message speaks to the Hispanic community as much as it does to the English-speaking community. Today, Lakewood is recognized as the fifth largest Hispanic church in the United States.[57]

COALO ZEMORANO

Marcos brought Coalo Zemorano onto the music staff to direct the choir during the Hispanic service. Many of the songs sung during the Hispanic service are Spanish translations of songs written by Cindy and Israel. Coalo is a native of Guadalajara, Mexico. His band, VCV—Vida Camino y Verdad (Life Way and Truth)—has performed in Mexico, Argentina, Colombia, Costa Rica, and El Salvador. In addition, he serves as vice president of the CanZion recording label. Coalo has also produced a children's album, which was nominated for a Latin Grammy in 2001.

LAKEWOOD'S BEST-KEPT SECRET

Together, the team at Lakewood is probably the greatest ministerial team in America. When people ask how Lakewood Church has grown from six thousand to over forty thousand people in seven years, the answer is really quite simple—the team that Joel Osteen has built and surrounded himself with.

If you want to build a great church, or organization of any kind, the secret is to find the most talented people you can and then allow them to do what they do. One of the things that many pastors and other leaders do not understand is that it is better to leave a position unfilled than to fill that position with the wrong person. When the wrong person has a job, he can damage the situation because of his lack of ability, leaving even greater problems later when he must be replaced with the right person for the job.

Joel Osteen does not get enough credit for the skill he has shown in putting together the leadership team of Lakewood Church. Critics want to focus on his lack of seminary training or pulpit experience, but he is not the first, even in recent times, to have a lack of formal education but succeed beyond expectations. Bill Gates, Steve Jobs, and Michael Dell are only three examples of individuals who dropped out of college and succeeded. Knowing how to build a great team is not a skill taught in most colleges or seminaries, but it is one of the most essential in building a great church, and Joel Osteen has demonstrated that skill well.

chapter thirteen

JOEL'S VISION FOR SUNDAYS

I have become all things to all men, that I might by
all means save some.
—1 Corinthians 9:22

O ur vision for the church is to help people reach their full potential in the things of God," Joel Osteen says. "The vision for the music is to reinforce what I preach. The music is positive. It's uplifting. It's fun."[58]

REACHING A DEMOGRAPHIC

These words, spoken in an interview, summarize the vision that Joel has brought to Lakewood. Even though it would appear that he did not plan to become the pastor of Lakewood, all throughout his life, God was instilling within him a vision for what Lakewood could become. As a television producer and marketing director for the church, he knew what kinds of things would get the attention of people and create a response to the gospel. In television, you must grab the attention of people in the first few moments or they will change the channel. Joel knew that in a church service the same principle would apply. What happens in the first few minutes of the service must grab the attention of people and then prepare them for what is ahead. The first minutes not only gain the attention of the viewer; they also create within them a desire to see what will happen during the rest of the program.

The way Joel has shaped the service at Lakewood is very much like the pattern of a television program. There are definite ebbs and flows to the service. Joel understands that people have a limited attention span. Also, there needs to be a certain level of quality in order to keep them watching the program. As it moves from song to greeting, praise and worship to prayer time, final song to offering, and special music to worship, the Lakewood service is totally geared toward keeping the attention of the audience by making the greatest impact possible. Joel's vision is to create a pattern to the service that the people can best respond to, but also to maintain a quality to which people can be drawn.

JOEL'S VISION IS TO CREATE A PATTERN TO THE SERVICE THAT PEOPLE CAN BEST RESPOND TO, WHILE MAINTAINING THE QUALITY.

The music of Lakewood helps to set it apart. The theme of the music fits in with the messages Joel brings from the pulpit. This is a part of Joel Osteen's vision. He understands that the theme of the service must run from the first note of the service to the last amen of dismissal. It would not be an easy task to find music to fit with each specific spoken message. But at Lakewood, Joel has brought the people on staff who can create that music. The music not only has words that proclaim the theme of the Lakewood services, but also the quality of the music is award-winning.

When John Osteen was pastor, Lakewood was already a very large church, a megachurch, with people of all ages attending. But, by far, the largest demographic in the church was older people, closer in age to John and Dodie. These were individuals and families who had been a part of Lakewood Church for a number of years and held positions of responsibility. Joel knew that for the church to grow there would have to be an emphasis on reaching younger people with children and teenagers. The church had to make an effort to reach out and build a strong group of younger adults.

This is something every television producer in America knows. Television networks crave the eighteen to forty-nine demographic. That is why the programs feature so many attractive young people. This is the audience being sought.

Joel wanted to build a service that would appeal to these families with children and teenagers, families who needed to be touched by the positive Word of God both in Houston and around the country. Joel built a staff of young, attractive, talented people who worked hard to reinforce the sermon

JOEL WANTED TO BUILD A SERVICE THAT WOULD APPEAL TO YOUNG FAMILIES WITH CHILDREN AND TEENAGERS AS WELL AS TO OLDER PEOPLE.

in a way that would encourage families to accept the message being presented. To some detractors, this may seem contrived or secular in its approach. In truth, Joel has done what churches across the country seek to do, except he has done it better. Mainline denominations across the country are dying because their congregations are aging and not being replaced with younger families. They have had little success in developing programs and campaigns to attract these families. Lakewood was not dying, by any means, but it would not be what it is today without Joel's vision of attracting young families to the church.

On the Sunday Joel was named senior pastor, he spoke of the plans to build a new building for the youth. This was not because of any explosive growth happening within the church; rather, it spoke to his acknowledgement of the priorities of the church. It spoke of his vision to see the needs of the young people as a priority for the vision of Lakewood. The five-story building was completed before the former Compaq center was occupied. A large amount of time and resources were spent to insure that the physical environment of the children's ministries would be among the finest in the country.

This is part of the vision of Joel Osteen: put a program together that will attract the demographic that you desire the most. Organize the program in a manner to which that demographic can relate. Go out and recruit the people who are capable of providing excellence in that program. Such a pattern can be repeated successfully time after time. Successful television programs last for many years because they provide a quality product, week after week. It was Joel's vision to provide the best service possible every Sunday. Because Lakewood does this, it attracts the biggest audience in the country, both in person and on television.

CREATING A MESSAGE

The other part of the vision is Joel's message. The message is like a television script. The script must appeal to as wide an audience as possible, but must especially appeal to the demographic you are trying to reach. John preached an upbeat message of victory for Christians. He preached that Christians should be victorious in every area of their lives. They should live lives of prosperity in their homes, experience success in their careers, and raise children who care for their parents and love the Lord because of the faith they have received at home and at church.

People who attended Lakewood under the preaching and ministry of John Osteen understood that they were not under their circumstances; they were on top of them. They were overcomers through the saving power of Jesus Christ and through the miraculous power the Holy Spirit gives to the Spirit-filled. John knew that people would learn what was presented to them through the Word. He taught them for nearly forty years that, through the overcoming power of God, they could and would change the world.

JOEL'S DESIRE IS TO SPEAK TO THE NEEDS OF THE PEOPLE OF THE 21ST CENTURY—TO PRESENT THE MESSAGE IN SUCH A WAY AS TO APPEAL TO AS MANY AS POSSIBLE.

Joel learned from his father not only because he grew up under his ministry, but also by editing his father's sermons for television for those seventeen years. Even though he preached in his father's shoes for the first several months, he understood that he was not his father and could not preach in the same way his father did. He had to develop his own style and manner of preaching. But he also understood the type of messages he felt led by the Lord to preach. Joel wanted to be an encourager like his dad, but in his own style. This was his vision for his messages. Preach a message of encouragement for the people. Give them something that would give them strength to get through their week.

One of the complaints people have about church is that the messages preached are not relevant to their lives. Joel had a vision to speak to the needs of the people week after week, to give them encouragement for daily living as well as direction for how they can achieve the best God has for their lives.

To this end, Joel speaks about how people can deal with the stress and strains of everyday life, and how to deal with the relationships they have with their families, coworkers, and bosses. This gives the audience, both on television and in person, motivation to tune in next week.

Again, this may appear worldly to some, and no way to conduct church to others, but the truth is, all ministries have some kind of planned approach to reach the audience they seek to serve. There is a reason that many traditional churches start worship at 11:00 a.m. The time was set many years ago when farmers had to do their chores before they could come to church. Services had to be scheduled late enough to allow them the time they needed. In this way, the church accommodated its membership and marketed to their needs. Preaching about heaven flourished for many years because the congregations were filled with farmers and industrial workers who toiled from dawn to dusk and needed to look forward to a time when they wouldn't have to work so hard. It was a message that spoke to the needs of the people. Joel's vision was to speak to the needs of the people of the twenty-first century—to present the message in such a way as to appeal to as many people as possible.

REACHING THE WORLD

The last part of Joel's vision is to take this message to the world. Joel has a passion for souls that became ingrained as he traveled with his father. But Joel's vision is to reach them in a different way—through the television ministry. Joel is also doing this through "An Evening with Joel Osteen" in sports arenas around the country. There is already discussion of taking this approach to different countries and continents. Joel and his leadership team are also examining other opportunities to spread the gospel through such modern modes as web- and podcasting. The Internet has become the great communications tool that reaches around the world. Lakewood services are being webcast live every weekend, and when you consider the population of the world that speaks either English or Spanish, that means that much of the world can watch and understand these services. The Lakewood podcast rates as one of the top one hundred most popular podcasts on iTunes.[59]

Joel's vision is much like the apostle Paul's: *"I have become all things to all men, that I might by all means save some"* (1 Corinthians 9:22). The twenty-first century has opened doors to ministry that the apostles could never have believed. Joel has taken the message of Jesus Christ that he learned at the feet of his father, and has a vision to take it to the world.

It is the vision of Joel Osteen to reach the world with the good news of Jesus Christ in a way that people can receive and understand, through any means possible. He is doing this better than anyone in the world at the present time. To those who do not approve of the message or method of Joel Osteen, this may be upsetting. But the fact is, thousands of people are accepting this message of good news and receiving Jesus Christ as their Lord and Savior. After all, isn't that what really matters?

chapter fourteen

JOEL AND VICTORIA

To whom much is given, from him much will be required.
—Luke 12:48

A t the time of John's death, no one could have predicted that Joel and Victoria Osteen would transition
so naturally into their leadership roles in the largest
church in the nation. Not even the family members who stood
behind them on Vision Sunday would have predicted that Joel
would step forward. At first appearance, they seem like the
ideal Christian couple, but they have their share of challenges
like anyone else.

FAIRYTALE ROMANCE?

Joel and Victoria's meeting was like a fairy tale. On CNN's
Larry King Live, Joel explained how he had stepped into a jewelry store to purchase a new battery for his watch. There he
met the most beautiful girl he had ever seen, a "fair maiden"
named Victoria.[60]

While Victoria sold him a new battery for his watch, and a
whole new watch as well, they began to talk, and Joel discovered that she was an active Christian. He thought to himself

that this was good, because if she had not been a Christian, he would have had to convert her! Victoria had been raised in the Church of Christ but had switched to a nondenominational church as a teenager. She had attended the University of Houston for two years before going to work in her family's jewelry store. Joel decided to pursue this to see if Victoria was the one God had for him.

Joel wasted no time in inviting her to a Houston Rockets basketball game at the Compaq Center in downtown Houston. He had season tickets and knew this would be a good opportunity for them to get to know each other. But after Victoria had accepted his invitation, he discovered that he had already given the tickets for that particular game to a friend of his earlier in the season. Joel's choice was to forget the ball game or buy tickets from a scalper outside of the arena. He decided to purchase tickets from a scalper. As Joel and Victoria tried to enter the Compaq Center, he discovered the tickets he had purchased from the scalper were for a game on another night. Joel went back to the scalper and, after some discussion, obtained tickets for that night's game. Their seats in the "nosebleed section" near the rafters were not as good as the ones he normally had with his season tickets, but at least they were inside the arena.

Around them was a group of young men who were enjoying the ball game, as well as a few beers. One of the men in the group was selected to go down to the court at halftime to attempt a half-court shot for a prize. When the young man made the half-court shot, his friends threw their hands up in excitement, launching their beer into the air. Joel earnestly prayed that when the beer fell, it would land on him and not on Victoria. This prayer was not answered. Joel didn't receive a drop, but Victoria was soaked in beer. This was not the fairy-tale moment Joel had been hoping for—the preacher's son taking his date home smelling like a brewery![61]

A GOOD COMPLEMENT

Joel Osteen is a man with precise routines; he is extremely structured and organized. This attention to detail has served him well as a television producer through the years. He gets up at the same time every day. He does the same things, maintains the same schedule, from week to week. He often goes to the same restaurants and eats the same food without even looking at the menu! Victoria is the opposite. She does not like routine; she prefers variety. Outgoing and energetic, adventurous and daring, there is no telling what Victoria is going to do next. The couple has found that this difference in their personalities has served both of them very well. Joel has become a little less structured because of Victoria. He is more open to new ideas and ways of doing things. Victoria now strives to fit within a structure when the situation demands it. They complement each other and make each other stronger.

LIFE AT HOME

Home life for the Osteens is as typical as the life of a nationally known pastor can be. They live in a fashionable, heavily wooded neighborhood on Houston's west side. Their house, purchased long before Joel became senior pastor of Lakewood, has recently been appraised at $2.3 million dollars, but cost Joel and Victoria $380,000 originally.[62] The value of their home has caused some criticism, but most of that criticism was deflected when it was revealed that Joel had stopped taking a salary from the church as soon as his book became a best seller.

Victoria has been Joel's biggest supporter since the very beginning. She was the first person to believe that Joel could be pastor of Lakewood. "I don't think I'd be where I am today if it was not for her encouragement, her vision," Joel has said. "You know, to me it's important, as husband and wife, that we build each other up, and she's always done that for me."[63]

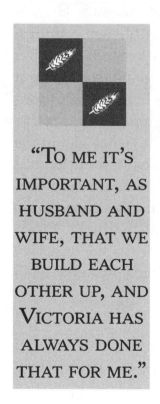

"TO ME IT'S IMPORTANT, AS HUSBAND AND WIFE, THAT WE BUILD EACH OTHER UP, AND VICTORIA HAS ALWAYS DONE THAT FOR ME."

Victoria has become one of the most recognized women in Christian television. She continues to be a true copastor in deed as well as title. Generally she addresses the congregation twice each Sunday, once with Joel during the welcome portion of the service, and then to introduce the offering. In the middle of each service, Victoria joins Joel and the rest of the Osteen family and counselors as they pray for people in need. In introducing the offering portion of the service, Victoria never makes it a time of begging or pressuring people to contribute. It is a time of teaching from the Word of God. Sometimes she will teach on the principles of seed faith—that God has ordained certain principles that guide our world, and if we want to receive a harvest, there must be a time of planting. Or, Victoria will teach other spiritual principles. This may seem like a small role, but how many other copastors, or pastors' wives, have the opportunity to impact more than forty thousand people each week, not to mention all those watching on television?

Victoria not only addresses the congregation every week, but she has also become a much-sought-after speaker for groups and churches outside of Lakewood. She speaks in cities across the country at Joel's live events, "An Evening with Joel Osteen." She appears with Joel to sign books at bookstores and retail outlets across the country. She often makes appearances with him in media interviews, such as CNN's *Larry King Live*. She has spoken at conferences, was featured in *The Church Report* magazine, and has a number of different sets of sermon series that she has completed in the Lakewood bookstore.

Together Joel and Victoria are one of the most influential couples in American evangelical Christianity. Pastors generally understand the value of having a highly visible spouse, even if her role is merely to stop gossip. Victoria has developed a reputation and a following of her own.

Making Family a Priority

Despite their very busy ministry lives, to Joel and Victoria, family comes first. They have two children, Jonathan and Alexandra, now eleven and seven, and work at keeping their family together as much as possible. When they travel to various cities for live events or speaking engagements, they take their children with them. Joel explained, "We do the events on Fridays; [they] get out of school Thursday at 2:00 o'clock, and so they miss one day of school, and the school's real good about it. We did twenty-two nights last year in different cities, and it's important to me that my kids are there with us. We hang out the day before, and they take part in the event."[64]

Alexandra will sometimes sing at these events, and Jonathan will often play a role as well. At one event he repeated the mantra that Joel starts every sermon with, and then he ended with the family's traditional tagline, "You sound great as usual."[65]

It is difficult to keep kids grounded when they are in the spotlight as much as Jonathan and Alexandra are, but Joel and Victoria are trying. One of the mistakes that pastors sometimes make with their own children is that they fail to help their children build a faith to call their own. Joel and Victoria are trying to avoid this pitfall.

EVERY DECISION JOEL AND VICTORIA MAKE AND EVERYTHING THEY DO MUST TAKE THE REALITY OF THE NATIONAL SPOTLIGHT INTO ACCOUNT.

Joel does most of his studying at home, allowing him to be there when his kids get home from school. Joel often uses his family as examples in his sermons and talks about how he and Victoria use positive words with their children. They often remind their children that they can do anything they want with their lives. They pray with them and help them to build their own faith in a personal way. Being home allows Joel to give his kids the attention they need at this point in their lives. It also helps that the kids have a lot of extended family around them. Cousins, both grandmothers, and a host of aunts and uncles have a strong presence in their lives.

Living in a pastor's home can be a real fishbowl existence. Living in the home of the pastor of the largest church in

America only enlarges the fishbowl. The Osteen children seem to accept the situation well. Recently Jonathan wrote in a school paper about what he wanted to do with his life. The last thing he mentioned was to pastor Lakewood.[66] Joel mentioned in a sermon how he and Jonathan were driving by the former Compaq Center before Lakewood moved in. Joel said to Jonathan that maybe one day he could preach in that arena. Jonathan, without hesitation, told his father that it was his ambition to preach at the Reliant Center, present home of the Houston Texans NFL team with a seating capacity of nearly four times that of the Compaq Center.[67] It certainly looks as though there is another generation of Osteen pastors being raised at Lakewood.

LIFE IN THE SPOTLIGHT

Joel and Victoria live in a kind of spotlight that few other pastors in the country have had to endure. Like all fairy tales, there is always the inevitable bump in the road. In December 2005, the Osteen family boarded a plane on their way to a ski vacation in Vail, Colorado. What happened next has been the fodder of hundreds of publications that have tried to retell the story. Apparently a liquid was spilled onto one of the seats they were assigned. Victoria wanted the spill cleaned before she would take her seat. Details of the story have been debated by all sides, but either the spill wasn't cleaned by the flight attendant, or it wasn't cleaned to Victoria's satisfaction. In the end, the Osteens had to leave the plane and take another flight. A church spokesman indicated that the family left the plane voluntarily, although an FBI spokesman told reporters that the Osteens were asked to leave the jetliner after "an altercation." Continental Airlines issued a statement indicating that there were "no remaining issues between Continental and those passengers." The FBI determined that there was nothing worth investigating.[68]

In a letter posted on the Lakewood website, Victoria stated,

> Regardless of how some have portrayed the situation, please know that it was truly a minor misunderstanding and did not escalate into what you saw or read in the news. Contrary to those reports, it was my choice to remove myself from the situation. Nonetheless, it was a most unfortunate event and I truly regret that it happened....The last thing I would ever want to do is let any of you down. And I promise you that I did not act in any way that would cast a bad light on you, my family, Lakewood Church, or our Lord Jesus Christ. I value the position that God has placed me in and I can assure you that I will always walk in love and integrity. While I am not perfect, I will always seek to be a peacemaker and seek the high road.[69]

Whether Victoria was simply a mother trying to care for her family, or a weary traveler dealing with her own frustrations, is hard for anyone who was not there to say. But the hard truth for Joel and Victoria is that they live in a much different world than did John Osteen. In today's reality of "on demand" news and Internet access, any public situation involving any person of "fame" is instantly flashed around the world, becoming the subject of tabloids, cable news, Internet blogs, and hundreds of other websties.

Joel said the situation was overblown, and that may be the case. But not many people are prepared for what happens when everything they do is instantly placed beneath the microscope of public opinion for the world to view, dissect, and critique. Today, Joel and Victoria live their lives as fair game for every person in America who either likes or dislikes them. When they make a mistake, critics will declare this to be proof that they are not the Christians they claim to be. Rarely do these same critics give any credit for the great things the Osteens have done for thousands of people. This is not necessarily fair, but it comes with the territory of pastoring the largest church in America, having the largest television ministry, being a *New York Times* best-selling author, and having the ability to fill huge sporting arenas across the nation. Joel and Victoria accept this as a part of their lives for the foreseeable future. Every decision Joel and Victoria make and everything they do must take this reality into consideration. If they fail to do this, it could have a major impact upon their lives and ministry. *"To whom much is given, from him much will be required"* (Luke 12:48) carries a lot of meaning for them.

A LOVE THAT LASTS

Joel is fortunate to have had a strongly grounded family life as a child. This has prepared him to build a strong family life with Victoria and their children today. Both of them were raised in Christian homes and have had a long relationship with the Lord. These realities are their greatest insurance toward weathering the problems of life. Hopefully, they will follow the example of Billy and Ruth Graham, who raised children and served God beneath the spotlight for sixty years. It has been done. It is possible.

For now, they are on top of the world, and it seems that everything they touch turns to gold. But, there may be times when things don't go so well in the future. Perhaps not every book will be a best seller. Or, maybe the arenas will no longer be full, and additional nights will not be scheduled. Another television ministry may come along and replace them as the favorite of the masses. If these times come, how will they deal with it as a couple? If adversity strikes, will it make their relationship stronger, or will it create wedges between them?

How well they will deal with future opportunities, as well as the trials of life, remains to be seen. Joel and Victoria give every impression of having a strong and healthy relationship, but nobody can say how the pressures of public life and ministry will affect their private lives. Joel and Victoria are having a major impact upon Christianity in America today, and as time goes by, they could very well have a major impact beyond the borders of this country, even more than they are doing today.

chapter fifteen

THE OSTEEN FAMILY

And because He loved your fathers, therefore He chose their
descendants after them; and He brought you out of Egypt
with His Presence, with His mighty power.
—Deuteronomy 4:37

A s Joel was appointed the leader of Lakewood Church, perhaps the biggest asset he had was the strength and support of the full Osteen family. His mother, Dodie, was very visible to the congregation for the first several years. As cofounder of the church, this visible support was important to reassure those members who had been a part of Lakewood for many years. Lisa has continued on as a staff member, and her leadership role has become more visible. Paul Osteen had been working as a surgeon in Little Rock, but he moved back to Houston and joined the leadership team of the church to support Joel. As mentioned earlier, Gary and April moved to the Dallas area in January 2000 to plant a church; Tamara and Jim were called to a pastorate in Victoria, Texas.

A BRIDGE FROM PAST TO PRESENT

Dodie's support for Joel as pastor cannot be overestimated. She is the bridge from the founding of the church at the feed store in 1959 to the new generation over forty years later. When John died, Dodie conducted his funeral and announced who would be preaching on future Sundays following John's death. Dodie was the one who announced to the congregation that Joel had been chosen to be the new senior pastor.

But Dodie Osteen represents more than just a public figure to Joel and Lakewood. She was copastor and cofounder of Lakewood Church with John. For forty years, she stood by John's side as he met everyone from politicians to prominent people in the charismatic and Pentecostal movements. Dodie led women's conferences for many years at Lakewood, hosting prominent women in the charismatic movement, and spoke at many conferences herself. While John was alive, it was Dodie who directed the services. John would say about her active involvement, "Dodie is half this ministry or more. I can go anywhere in the world, and Dodie can take care of the church."[70]

PERHAPS THE BIGGEST ASSET JOEL HAS IS THE STRENGTH AND SUPPORT OF THE ENTIRE OSTEEN FAMILY.

After John died, Dodie did not ever presume to become permanent senior pastor, but she was very obviously the head of the pulpit search committee. For all practical purposes, she was the interim pastor between John and Joel. The congregation looked to her as a link between the past leadership of John and the path to the future leadership of the church. Without the visible presence of Dodie Osteen, the transition from the pastoral leadership of John to the leadership of their son Joel would have been difficult, if not impossible. Dodie has earned her own credentials as a leader in the charismatic movement. In fact, she was given an honorary doctorate by Oral Roberts University on May 4, 1991.

Dodie is highly respected and beloved by the entire city of Houston. A few months after John died, she was invited to throw out the first pitch for the Houston Astros. She told the press that she wasn't Randy Johnson but was thrilled and very surprised to participate. She said that she had to practice since she hadn't thrown a baseball since her children were little.[71]

For several years after Joel was named senior pastor, Dodie continued to address the congregation at every service. She spoke at The Compaq Center celebration weekend, speaking of how the move fulfilled John's vision and dreams. A few weeks after the move into The Compaq Center, Dodie withdrew from participation at each weekend service. She still attends every weekend, and members of the congregation can still catch a glimpse of her on the monitors during prayer. She also continues to conduct monthly healing services for those who wish to come for a time of prayer for healing.

THE OSTEEN PRESENCE

The board of directors of Lakewood is made up entirely of members of the Osteen family. They make all the major decisions for the church, with the assistance of staff members and paid advisors brought in to provide expertise with specific situations. The Osteens truly believe that Lakewood Church is a sacred trust of which they have been made stewards.

With Paul Osteen and Lisa Comes, along with her husband, Kevin, on staff, there was a foundation upon which the leadership team of Lakewood could be built to support

Joel and the ministry. One of Joel's first priorities, which he enunciated on Vision Sunday, was to take care of the needs of the members of Lakewood Church, and the family focuses on this. Other staff members may come and go, but the family is always present, always faithful, to meet the needs of the membership of Lakewood.

LISA COMES

Lisa Comes is not on staff just because she is family. She has been instrumental in the development of several of the ministries of the church. While attending Oral Roberts University, she met and fell in love with a young man, George Allen Jackson. They were married in 1981, and Lisa seemed to feel her life was set. George was planning to become a pastor, and Lisa felt comfortable with this because she had grown up in a pastor's home. From the beginning, however, their marriage began to experience problems. After they were married for two years, George asked Lisa for a divorce. Lisa was devastated and felt that her life was over.

She returned home and lived with her parents for the next six weeks. She didn't go to church or anywhere else. All she wanted to do was pull the covers over her head and make the world go away. She thought that God could never use her again. Even though John had been divorced, Lisa had always thought that marriage was forever and that Christians did not look well upon people whose marriages didn't last. She never really imagined herself as a preacher, but she always believed that she would be in ministry. Now she felt this was never to be.

The family wanted to help, but no one knew what to do. Lisa felt like a total failure. She felt she had let down her father,

her family, and Lakewood Church. Finally, John informed Lisa that it was time to go to church and share her needs with the people in her life. Not having a better plan, she agreed.

When John shared with the congregation that Lisa was hurting, and why, they began to place their arms around her and pray for her. They reached out to her with love and told her that God still loved her and so did the people of Lakewood. Other people in the church began to share with her the problems in their lives, and often the problems were in their relationships with spouses or children. Lisa saw that her divorce did not need to be the end of ministry for her. She began to see that God was opening a new door of ministry that she could never have imagined before.[72]

LISA BEGAN TO SEE THAT GOD WAS OPENING A NEW DOOR OF MINISTRY FOR HER THAT SHE COULD NEVER HAVE IMAGINED BEFORE.

During the dissolution of her first marriage, Lisa reached out to many married couples at Lakewood. She encouraged couples to work at their marriages and seek God as they tried to solve their problems. She was invited to speak at conferences and wrote articles and booklets about her experience. Lisa's belief in marriage and the work it takes to keep it intact was well-known throughout the congregation. She had persevered in prayer for her marriage, but, in the end, her marriage was not repaired, and there was no restoration or reconciliation.

This experience provided another way for Lisa and her family to understand the pain of divorce and its impact on families. It also gave them an understanding of the life of single adults in today's society. Lisa experienced the complete cycle. She was married, experienced the pain of marital separation and divorce, then lived as a single woman for an expanded period of time. Lisa developed a compassion for single adults and the challenges they face every day. She shared her insights with her extended family and allowed them to see that divorce and the pain it brings can come to any person, and any family.

This event, and others like it, served as evidence that the Osteen family was just like any other family. They weren't special. They experienced many of the same trials and tribulations that impact many families in our contemporary society.

One day, Lisa was going into a service and noticed a young man near the back row of the auditorium. She asked him to help her minister to people who were at the altar reaching out to the Lord. She had never met him, and she didn't know if he had any idea about how to help others in this way or not, but she just felt led by the Lord to speak to him. Lisa, like the other Osteen children, had learned to always obey the urging of the Lord. This young man turned out to be Kevin Comes, a successful businessman working as a project manager for TD Industries. Kevin had begun attending Lakewood Church in 1984 and over the years had volunteered in several ministries. Kevin and Lisa began dating in the fall of 1989 and were married in November of 1990. Shortly after they were married, John asked Kevin if he was interested in taking a position at the church. After much prayer, Kevin turned the offer down. He was involved with the building of a large bioscience facility for Texas A&M University at the Texas Medical Center in Houston. Nearly a year later, the project was completed and

Kevin felt it was the time to take the position at Lakewood. He spent the next seven years as facilities manager, as well as overseeing several construction projects and several sanctuary renovations.

In the fall of 1997, Justin Osteen resigned as church administrator to pursue a consulting business. After several weeks, Kevin assumed that position, where he continues to serve today. Kevin's previous experience as a building project manager proved invaluable to Lakewood as they planned to make the huge move into the former Compaq Center.

This was God's hand in motion. Nearly twenty years before Lakewood would step out to achieve one of the largest church relocation and building projects in the world, God brought a young man to Lakewood Church who would be perfectly prepared to meet that challenge. He brought this young man into the life of a young lady who was striving to serve the Lord amidst the challenges in her life. He then brought him onto the church staff just in time for him to step up to this major building challenge. There was no doubt in the minds of his family, the church staff, and the congregation that he was up to the challenge before them.

> THERE WAS NO DOUBT IN THE MINDS OF HIS FAMILY, THE CHURCH STAFF, OR THE CONGREGATION THAT KEVIN WAS UP TO THE CHALLENGE.

Kevin would be the point man in the entire project for the Compaq Center. As the point man, he was responsible for the following: putting together the Request for Proposal (RFP) that was submitted to the City of Houston, lobbying meetings with the Houston City Council members, working directly with the lobbying firm (Walden & Associates), working directly with the two law firms (Winstead, Sechrest & Minick and Fulbright & Jaworski), interviewing and hiring the project management firm for the project (IrvineDCS Team), interviewing and hiring the architectural firms for the project (Studio Red Architects and Morris Architects), and interviewing and hiring the general contractor for the project (Tellepsen Builders). Additionally, he led the Lakewood design team that met with the architects, engineers, and the twenty-five-plus consultants hired to design the facility.

Kevin and Lisa's marriage has not been without its own challenges. Unable to start a family, Lisa underwent several surgeries to correct the problem, yet still they were unable to conceive. Lisa again submitted to additional medical procedures, some of which were very stressful on her body and very expensive. Several thousands of dollars and seven years of time later, there was still no success. Finally, doctors told the couple that there would be no biological children in their life. Once again, the Osteen family faced one of the same challenges that many couples face today: infertility.

At that time, a woman from Lakewood, who was unaware of their situation, called them. She was in a ministry that took care of teens in trouble. She told them, "I've never done this before, but I have a young lady who is about to give birth to twin girls. Would you and Kevin like to adopt them?" Kevin and Lisa both recognized immediately that God was answering their prayers. Today the Comes family has three beautiful children, all adopted. And they understand better how to minister to people facing similar challenges in their lives.

Today both Kevin and Lisa speak to groups both at Lakewood and outside of the church. They have also written books and articles that minister to others. Lisa teaches nearly every week on Wednesday nights. In many ways, she is a more traditional preacher than Joel. Her preaching is very much like her father's preaching was; she gives messages of encouragement, but is likely to use more Bible verses and the retelling of biblical events to make her points.

PAUL OSTEEN

Paul Osteen and his wife, Jennifer, have five children: Matt, Georgia, Olivia, Sophia, and Jackson. After his father's death, Paul gave up a career as a surgeon and moved his family back to Houston to become a valued teacher at the church. When Paul told his mother about their call to return to Houston, she asked him what he wanted to do at Lakewood. His reply showed the humility of this skilled surgeon: "I have a tractor. I can mow the grass if you like."[73]

Two things can be said about Paul Osteen: he is a great encourager and a great team member. Paul has been there to reassure his younger brother through the many changes that have happened at Lakewood in the last seven years. He is a sounding board for his brother and backs him in all situations. When the media asks Paul about his brother, he never has anything but words of support and encouragement. Paul beams with excitement at what God is doing at Lakewood through the leadership of his brother. Joel, as well, speaks of his feelings for his brother from the pulpit almost every service.

Immediately after Joel assumed the position of senior pastor, Paul initiated a class for new Christians. This class has become an essential part of the growth of Lakewood Church. In the months after Joel became pastor, thousands of people walked the aisles to receive Jesus Christ as their Lord and Savior. But they needed to be discipled in the foundations of the faith. If this had not happened, Lakewood Church would have been just a revolving door where people came and went. These classes allow people to grow in their new faith. The growth of the church is evidence of the fruit from these classes.

Paul is also responsible, along with his sister Lisa, for the day-to-day operations of the church. Together they help to ensure that the weddings, funerals, and all the practical aspects of providing services that the people of Lakewood need as a part of their lives come off without a hitch.

chapter sixteen

WRITING A
BEST SELLER

That I might by all means save some.
—1 Corinthians 9:22

I n October 2004, Joel released his first book through Warner Faith, *Your Best Life Now: 7 Steps to Living at Your Full Potential.* Immediately, it debuted on the best-sellers lists. In the first six weeks, it sold seven hundred thousand copies.[74] By the end of seven weeks, a million copies had been sold.[75] Before the end of the year, less than three months after it had been released, the book was number one on the *New York Times* Best Sellers list for advice books. Joel embarked on a cross-country book tour soon after the book was released. The two-night appearance of "An Evening with Joel Osteen" at Madison Square Garden, just two weeks after the book's release, certainly didn't hurt the sales any.

Your Best Life Now took Joel's ministry into an entirely new market. Joel said of the seven steps listed in the book, "These are what I feel are the key things. If you don't have these right, you're going to have problems."[76] Joel included a number of stories about the Osteen family as well as other illustrations from the Bible and everyday life. The book reads much like the sermons that have made Joel the popular figure that he is. It wasn't complicated theology or even deep biblical lessons. He simply took Scripture and applied it to everyday life. The book gave readers a foundation from which they could build a better life.

Joel's four-day, seven-city book signing tour brought in record crowds and sold out books at every stop. Everywhere Joel went, there were thousands of people standing in lines at department and discount stores in major cities across the country. Joel did not always go to the major bookstores. He also appeared at Wal-Marts and Sam's Clubs, places where everyday people go to shop. At one personal appearance at a Wal-Mart, over twelve hundred books were sold. At another of Joel's Wal-Mart appearances, lines began to form at three o'clock in the morning. In the end, so many books were sold in the first two weeks that seven additional press runs were eventually needed.

Joel gave a number of interviews to both broadcast and print media across the country that promoted both the book and his live events in arenas around the nation. Joel discussed why he wrote the book: "My core message is a message of hope and encouragement. I think people are looking for that these days." When he was questioned about being so positive, Joel gave insight into his total ministry philosophy: "I just don't believe in condemning people and being judgmental. Yes, there's a way of condemning people and knocking them down and getting them to feel bad. That maybe can turn some people around, but I believe in just speaking the truth and letting them know they have good things in store. Some people don't like it when you're positive. However, we've seen thousands and thousands of lives changed, so I try not to focus on that."[77] He then summed the book up in a few words: "I think the whole thesis of the book is that you need to just bloom where you're planted."[78]

Joel seemed to take the entire media world by storm. ABC placed an extended excerpt from his book on its website after an interview on *Good Morning, America*. The book was obviously connecting with people all over the country. Joel seemed to be everywhere, both in person and through the media. Reporter John A. Zukowski described Joel as soft-spoken, with a kind of politeness that comes from genuine cheerfulness rather than celebrity charm. He wrote that, away from the TV lights, Joel seemed like a small-town pastor.[79] Several media members suggested that Joel had captured the broad appeal of Dr. Billy Graham.

AT ONE OF JOEL'S WAL-MART BOOK SIGNINGS, LINES BEGAN TO FORM AT THREE O'CLOCK IN THE MORNING.

Not every Christian media group or organization in the country greeted the book with wide acclaim. *Christianity Today* reviewed the book in less than glowing terms. The title of the article reviewing the book gave away the author's attitude, "Thou Shalt Not Be Negative." The reviewer ended with this sentence: "For readers who know the spiritual limits of health, prosperity, and even a positive attitude, the book of Ecclesiastes would be better reading."[80]

In 2005, *Your Best Life Now Journal* was released, designed to accompany the first book and allow individuals to record their thoughts on how the book was impacting their lives. The journal immediately began to sell in the hundreds of thousands. At the grand-opening weekend for the Compaq Center, *Your Best Life Now Devotional* was prereleased, and a copy was given to every family in attendance.

Your Best Life Now has become its very own brand, much like Rick Warren's *Purpose Driven Life* books. Warner Faith publisher Rolf Zettersten discussed the success of Joel's book and their marketing strategy. "I'm being very careful about not over-publishing Joel. I think Joel is going to have a very long career as an author, and so we'd like to be very deliberate, very strategic about what he's publishing. We could have done a book for graduation, a book for moms or for dads, but felt that would really be too much exploitation and we just really wanted to guard his long-term publishing prospects."[81]

Joel's presence and potential in the publishing world brought him an unusual contract for his next book. In March 2006, Joel signed a contract with Free Press, an imprint of Simon & Schuster, to publish his next book some time in 2007. The contract was unusual because instead of the usual advance and the industry-standard royalty rate of 15 percent, Joel's contract gives him a smaller advance, perhaps one or two million dollars, and then a full 50 percent of the publisher's profit on sales.[82]

Through his book, and its spin-offs, Joel has had the opportunity to touch the lives of thousands of people that he would not have been able to reach any other way. People in an airport bookstore or Sam's Club will see his book, glance through it, and likely buy a copy. Then at home, in a private moment, God may use the book to reach out and touch their lives. Because of the impact of the book, they may turn on the television and, on BET or The Family Channel, they may watch the Lakewood television broadcast and respond to an invitation to accept Jesus Christ as Lord and Savior.

Again, as the apostle Paul said, *"To the weak I became as weak, that I might win the weak. I have become all things to all men, that I might **by all means** save some"* (1 Corinthians 9:22, emphasis added). Joel is using a marvelous worship service, broadcast all over the world, and adding to that books, tapes, ministry outreaches, and public appearances, all designed to touch as much of the world as possible. The media recognizes this reality when they write such things as, "The groundswell of people turning to Osteen shows he's reaching the massive audience between non-religious cynics and far-right extremists."[83] This was Joel's hope when he wrote the book. He said as much in an interview: "It's been a very pleasant surprise that the message has crossed over into the whole community, because we never wanted to reach just the Christian community. We've reached them, and we keep talking to them and it just feels like that we ought to get beyond the church borders."[84]

It's hard to deny the fact that Joel Osteen is proving himself to be one of the great marketing geniuses in the history of the Christian world. Not only does he lead the largest Protestant church in America, with the largest audience of any Christian television broadcaster in the country, but now he also has sold out live events at major sporting arenas around the country, and has a best-selling book that has been on the *New York Times* Best Sellers list for over eighteen months. No one else has ever come close to what Joel has accomplished. Church, TV, live tours, a national best seller—he is not the first to attempt this quadruple play, but he has done it more successfully than anyone else. John Hagee has a large church in San Antonio, Texas, and has written books that have been widely received, but he's never seriously impacted the secular markets. Robert Schuller's Crystal Cathedral, in Los Angeles, would probably be a close second in doing what Joel is doing, but his church is not nearly as large, and he has never filled out-of-town arenas. Only Joel knows if all this was a part of his plan when he became pastor in 1999, or if even he has been astounded by the way his life has unfolded over time.

JOEL OSTEEN IS PROVING HIMSELF TO BE ONE OF THE GREAT MARKETING GENIUSES IN THE HISTORY OF THE CHRISTIAN WORLD.

The real question that must be asked is this: what impact will the success of *Your Best Life Now,* as well as the books to come, have on Joel and the ministry of Lakewood? The kind of money this book continues to earn for Joel could change the life of any man. Only he and his family can know how they will deal with this vast fortune. It is estimated that Joel has earned in excess of ten million dollars in royalties for the books he has written up to 2006.[85] When *Your Best Life Now* goes paperback, and his next book is published, his earnings will climb even higher. This is the kind of fortune that the vast majority of Americans can only imagine.

When the success of the book took off, Joel announced that he would no longer accept a salary from Lakewood Church. This was an admirable gesture, but not a tremendous sacrifice. After all, his church salary of two hundred thousand dollars a year would not even begin to pay the taxes on his vast book income. When Rick Warren began to earn millions of dollars from his book, *The Purpose Driven Life*, he not only stopped receiving a salary from the church, but he also paid back to the church all the money he had ever received in salary. Joel has not been a pastor very long, so a similar gesture would not be that significant.

Neither Joel nor Victoria was raised in poverty. They have been successful in their investment ventures during their marriage. They are co-owners of a television station, no small thing itself. It will be interesting to see how they deal with such a huge influx of cash.

Success brings with it the glare of the spotlight. The final analysis is this: Joel's position as a national best-selling author has the potential to be a very positive force in his life and ministry, and it has the potential to become a huge distraction that could lead to his downfall. Which of these two results will happen rests with him and his family. One thing is sure—the world will be watching.

chapter seventeen

TALKING TO
THE PRESS

*Be sober, be vigilant; because your adversary the devil walks about
like a roaring lion, seeking whom he may devour.*
—1 Peter 5:8

J oel began doing interviews with the national broadcast
and print media, as well as the local media, while traveling across the nation doing book tours and conduct-
ing services in major sports arenas. As Joel soon learned, it
is the goal of many interviewers, particularly in the secular
press, to catch you saying something that can create a national
headline. It becomes a feather in their hat if their interview
can become a story of its own—to have the rest of the world's
media say, "Joel Osteen said on CNN...on Fox News...on *The
Today Show*...on *Good Morning, America*, etc." It is not the job of
the interviewer to make Joel or anyone else look good. Their
only goal is to further their own careers. Most of the secular press has little or no understanding of evangelical Christianity, and even less of charismatic or Pentecostal churches.
An interviewer often comes into an interview assuming that
there is an "angle" or "hidden secret" to be exposed. Why else
would people be interested in what this pastor has to say?

This becomes obvious in the kinds of questions that are asked. They often reflect the reporter's lack of knowledge of the ways of God. The interviews are suspicious of anyone who would claim there is a God who does amazing things in the lives of people today.

Joel is certainly aware that in order to touch the world for Jesus outside the four walls of a church, you must venture beyond those walls to do it. Joel's journey beyond the walls of Lakewood has included being interviewed by all the major networks, both cable and broadcast. CBS news correspondent Byron Pitts described Joel as someone who looks like an anchorman, talks like a Southern salesman, and runs the congregation like a C.E.O. Pitts's interview focused on the amount of money that Lakewood receives in offerings, as well as the amount of money Joel was making from his book. [86]

When interviewed for *The CBS Early Show*, coanchor Harry Smith focused on the positive aspect of the message that Joel preaches. Smith claimed that after reading the book he thought that Joel's message seems to be about God and perhaps less about Christ than one might expect from an evangelical preacher. Smith also compared Joel to Norman Vincent Peale and asked Joel what he thought of the comparison. Joel agreed that some things between them were alike. Smith also asked Joel if he thought God was behind natural disasters like Hurricane Katrina. Joel replied that he believed that it was God who helped people through disasters.[87]

NBC interviewed Joel in a piece that appeared on *The Today Show*. Jamie Gangel, of MSNBC, did the interview. To those who liked Joel, it seemed that every question was designed to catch him in something that might become a headline. Gangel described Joel as more of a self-help guru than a preacher.

She played a previously taped interview with one of his critics and then asked Joel what he thought of the criticism. Gangel specifically quoted other things that critics were saying about Joel, such as his "watered-down Christianity" and his "cotton candy theology," and concluded by asking him if he knew why he was so popular. Joel tried to address these issues, but in such an abbreviated and heavily edited interview, he wisely avoided saying anything that could become a headline.[88]

A few weeks later, Tyler Mathisen of CNBC mentioned Joel in a piece about God and money and their relationship in the evangelical community. Joel was quoted as saying he thought the Lakewood broadcast and his book were making a difference in the lives of people who did not routinely attend church.[89]

When Joel's book was released, ABC News tried to create controversy by referring to another interview where Joel discussed whether non-Christians would go to heaven. He was also asked whether the faith of then Supreme Court nominee Harriet Miers should be considered in regard to her nomination to the court.[90] Several months later, ABC's

> IN ORDER TO TOUCH THE WORLD FOR JESUS OUTSIDE THE FOUR WALLS OF A CHURCH, YOU MUST VENTURE BEYOND THOSE WALLS.

Nightline did another piece on Joel. They described how Joel's ministry had changed since assuming the position of senior pastor at Lakewood. *Nightline* also interviewed critics who said they didn't like Joel's lack of public condemnation for people with sin in their lives.[91]

CONTROVERSY

But there is little doubt that the two interviews that created the most controversy around Joel were his interviews with CNN's Larry King and Fox News' Bill O'Reilly. Joel was interviewed on O'Reilly's program on Christmas Eve of 2004. O'Reilly questioned Joel's lack of formal theological education. He then asked Joel if people could live their full potential if they were agnostic or atheistic. When Joel said he didn't think so, O'Reilly followed that up by saying that many brilliant agnostics and atheists have made major contributions to society.

This is a typical tactic of interviewers. They ask a question to which any response will be wrong. If Joel had said that agnostics and atheists often make meaningful contributions, the entire evangelical world would have been offended because Joel didn't say that life could only be fully realized with a personal relationship with Jesus Christ. Joel attempted to diffuse the situation by answering that with Christ in our lives we can do even more. O'Reilly ended the interview by remarking that even though he had sold as many books as Joel had he felt that he was not as happy as Joel. One has to wonder if Bill O'Reilly ever considered the possibility that Joel's relationship with God could provide a foundation for his happiness.

But, by far, the interview that has created the most controversy for Joel was his interview with CNN's Larry King. Larry King tries to get his guest comfortable before the interview. When the guest is relaxed, King can quietly ask candid questions that will make headlines in the next morning's newspapers. King opened the interview mentioning that he had met John and Joel several years earlier at a function in

Houston. King then went through a variety of issues; each question could have been explosive depending upon Joel's answer. Are you a fire-and-brimstone preacher? Did you go to seminary? Are you really ordained? Can you marry people? Are you affiliated with a denomination? How do you raise the money for the church and the television broadcast? Do you agree with Billy Graham? Then King asked the question that made the headlines: who goes to heaven? What if you are Jewish or Muslim and have never accepted Christ?

Joel was being placed in the interviewer's web. Once again, it was a "no win" situation. If Joel said Jews and Muslims are going to hell because of their lack of a salvation experience, by morning his statements would be labeled as a "hate speech" and proof of Joel's divisiveness. If Joel indicated that they might go to heaven, evangelical Christians everywhere would condemn him. Joel tried to respond with an answer similar to one that Billy Graham had used the previous week on *The Larry King Show*—that it is not our place to judge. But then Joel went on to elaborate about having observed the sincerity of the different religions of India. He said that he knew that such religious people were sincere in their faith and would go to great lengths to prove their devotion. But he never plainly stated that they would not go to heaven. Such an incomplete answer and the lack of condemnation of other religious faiths caught the attention of the evangelical world.

King completed the interview by asking questions about same-sex marriage, whether we should apologize for slavery, and why God allows bad things like 9/11 to happen. He also inquired about Joel's book, about filling Madison Square Garden, and why they sold tickets to the events.

In the latter portion of the broadcast, calls were taken from viewers. Some callers admired Joel and some wanted to ask him biblical questions that would have taken a considerable amount of time and preparation to answer. The interview ended with Victoria joining Joel on the set. King asked Victoria questions about how she and Joel met and remarked on how pretty he thought she was.[92]

Before they were even off the air, the Internet was ablaze with bloggers criticizing Joel for his answer about who would go to heaven. Within days Joel felt the need to place an apology on the Lakewood website for any misunderstanding and assured the world that he believed that salvation could only be obtained through Jesus Christ.

MEGACHURCH TARGETS

The print press is fascinated with megachurches and often uses Lakewood as the largest and greatest example. The fascination centers on the way in which megachurches are run like a business with marketing campaigns and demographic studies. *Business Week* ran an interview with Joel asking him about his approach to reaching his audience.[93] The *Christian Science Monitor* quoted Joel in an article entitled, "The Rise of the American Megachurch." The article focused on how religious rituals and symbols have been replaced by bands and upbeat music.[94] Perhaps the most positive article in the country about Joel and Lakewood appeared in the *Washington Post*. They labeled Joel, "The Smiling Preacher," a label that has been repeated in both the print and broadcast media all over the country.[95] There have also been glowing articles in the *New York Times*. One of the realities in our nation today is that if you want to be taken seriously in the society of the ruling elite, you must be well regarded by these two newspapers. The power of these two papers cannot be questioned.

The Christian media seems to be divided into two camps. Those who are sympathetic to the charismatic and Word of Faith movements regard Joel as successfully changing the face of Christianity. They applaud the success of his ministry and his finances. The remainder of the Christian media tends not to be as sympathetic. They question the theological foundation of Joel's sermons as well as his style.

LAKEWOOD CHURCH HAS EXPERIENCED MORE GROWTH IN ATTENDANCE AND IN CONVERSIONS THAN SOME ENTIRE EVANGELICAL GROUPS HAVE.

In some ways, there seems to be as much partisanship in the Christian world as there is in the political world. The undeniable truth is that Lakewood Church has experienced more growth in attendance and in conversions than some entire evangelical denominations. Between Lakewood's services in Houston and those around the country, the number of people confessing to believe in Jesus Christ through the ministry of Joel Osteen reaches into the hundreds of thousands. Still, many in the Christian media would label Joel as something less than a believer. Joel does not say the things they would like him to say in the way they would like him to say them. Joel does not stay within what they believe the established box of Christianity should be. Joel breaks out of the box by using the secular media to reach an audience that cannot be reached any other way. He reaches people who do not watch Christian television or read Christian magazines, people who do not walk into churches for religious services other than weddings or funerals. He understands that to reach the world we must reach those outside the normal scope of the church.

It is difficult to distinguish those who first heard of Joel and Lakewood by channel surfing, picking up his book, or by seeing an interview in the media, since his message is saturating the marketplace. Joel wants only to open the minds of people to consider their need for a relationship with Jesus Christ. He always encourages people to become a part of a Bible-believing church where they can grow into a mature relationship with the Lord. The world can continue to scrutinize and question the success of Lakewood Church and Joel Osteen. But hundreds of thousands of changed lives in Houston and in cities across the United States will continue to answer the question for him.

chapter eighteen

An Evening with Joel Osteen

*You shall be witnesses to Me in Jerusalem, and in all Judea and
Samaria, and to the end of the earth.*
—Acts 1:8

I n the summer of 2004, Joel and Victoria began a tour of
some of the nation's largest and best-known sports arenas. The first stop was Atlanta's Philips Arena on Friday
night, July 9. Duncan Dodds said that the goal was to create
some "face time" with the millions who watch Lakewood's
weekly television show and only experience Joel and Lakewood Church from their living rooms.[96] The events were simply called, "An Evening with Joel Osteen." When Lakewood
announced the services, they also announced that they would
be full Lakewood services including Cindy Cruse-Ratliff,
Israel Houghton, a one-hundred-ten-voice choir, and the Lakewood orchestra. Dodie, Victoria, and Paul would speak to the
audience in addition to Joel.

Stepping out of the comfort zone of East Houston for the
first time was a big step for Joel and the Lakewood team. Some
would think it arrogant to rent a large arena about eight hundred miles away from home and expect people to come and

fill it. But one man's arrogance is another man's faith. Joel and his team wanted to make a difference in the entire country, not just in Houston. Joel had traveled thousands of miles to many foreign lands when he worked with his father. He had witnessed his father's passion to reach people for Jesus. When Joel became pastor he made the commitment to reach people here at home. Traveling the country and speaking in arenas was one way of keeping that commitment. Joel expressed his feelings very directly: "Two or three years ago, I felt that we should go into cities because we have a good TV following and we wanted to touch people there in their own city. But I didn't know what to expect or what size of arena to get. So we just decided to step out in faith and just get a big one."[97]

No tickets were sold for Philips Arena in Atlanta, but the turnstiles counted 19,235 people in attendance for the service. At least three thousand people had to be turned away from the arena despite some having traveled from as far away as Tennessee, North and South Carolina, and Florida. Free booklets by Joel were quickly distributed to the disappointed fans.[98] A few weeks later they repeated the process in Anaheim, California. Again thousands had to be turned away.

The next challenge was one of the biggest: New York City. They say, if you can make it there, you can make it anywhere. In October 2005, Joel and the Lakewood team arrived in New York for two evenings at Madison Square Garden. But the New York event would be different. In view of the fact that they turned away crowds in Atlanta and Anaheim, and at the urging of the Madison Square Garden management, a decision was made to sell tickets to the services.

This provided a great deal of comment and controversy around the country. Later when Joel and Victoria were on

CNN's *Larry King Live,* a caller complained about their selling tickets. She said a number of people from her church wanted to attend but could not afford to purchase tickets. The reason for tickets was pragmatic, not financial. There had to be a way to control the number of people who showed up for the services.

It's one thing to have people surrounding Philips Arena in Atlanta and Arrowhead Pond in Anaheim, but a crowd of angry New Yorkers unable to get in was not something the Madison Square Garden officials wanted to experience. "They called us [from] Madison Square Garden and said, 'You must ticket this event. It will be mayhem if you don't,'" said Don Iloff.[99] Tickets could have been given away, but what would stop people from getting a hundred tickets for a church group and only using thirty of them? By selling tickets for ten dollars, most people could afford them if they wanted to come, and it seemed to be enough money to make people attend once they had purchased the tickets. At ten dollars a ticket, "An Evening with Joel Osteen" sold out Madison Square Garden twice.

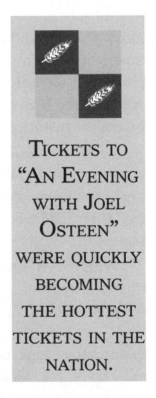

TICKETS TO "AN EVENING WITH JOEL OSTEEN" WERE QUICKLY BECOMING THE HOTTEST TICKETS IN THE NATION.

The services in New York were held shortly after Joel's book was released. Hundreds of people came to New York to buy a copy of the book, stand in line at a bookstore personal appearance for an autograph, and then line up outside the Garden to attend the service. Joel and the team knew that filling "the Garden" in New York was a big deal. Paul Osteen remarked,

"It is such a historic place. There is something about coming to the biggest city in America. I'm just overwhelmed by the support and enthusiasm. New York City and Madison Square Garden, it is almost a gateway to the world. I think this will just validate the impact of Joel's ministry to the nation."[100]

A DVD was made of the Madison Square Garden event. It was the talk of the country, both in the Christian and secular media.[101] Joel and the team gave New York the full Lakewood experience. Cindy Cruse-Ratliff and Israel Houghton led the praise and worship, the orchestra belted out the music, and one hundred fifty choir members paid their own way to be a part of the historic services.

After New York, the tour was just getting started. In Dallas, Joel and the team sold out the American Airlines Center. There is a big rivalry between Dallas and Houston, but even the Dallas media could not deny the popularity of Joel's message.[102]

Within two weeks of the Dallas event, the team went to Charlotte, North Carolina. There, the local media sarcastically reported that Joel could do what their local NBA team, the Charlotte Bobcats, could not do: fill the Charlotte Coliseum. Twenty-two thousand people crowded into the arena to get a glimpse of Joel, Victoria, and the Lakewood worship experience. Charlotte was the first to report scalpers selling tickets far in excess of their face value. Different ticket agencies across the country began to announce that tickets to "An Evening with Joel Osteen" were among the hottest tickets in the nation. Tickets to see Joel were in greater demand than many of the big musical acts in the country.

After sell-out appearances in Miami and Oakland, Joel and the team went to Chicago where he came to the attention of the *Chicago Sun-Times* when a reader angrily e-mailed the religion editor decrying the fact that some people were scalping tickets for as much as $190. The indignant reader wrote, "Have these people no morals? No conscience? They are selling $10 tickets for an event dedicated to God and prayer for a hundred bucks or more!! Truly sinful!"[103] The newspaper was unfamiliar with evangelists who sold tickets to their services. They noted that neither Billy Graham nor Benny Hinn had ever charged for services. Hinn's ministry had to give tickets away the last time he was in town.

The ticket-scalping story in the *Sun-Times* caught the attention of the Southern Baptists. Mary Knox of *The Baptist Standard* wrote an editorial regarding the situation. In the essay, he covered the paradoxical way that many Baptists saw the situation:

> Many Baptists rush to find fault with Osteen's ministry. Some of the criticism is valid. We're leery of charismatic religion; we've seen abuses. We point to gospel themes of sin and justice; faith isn't all sweetness and light. And we note the shallowness of big-event religion; the local church is where people are discipled, ministry happens and community takes place. Still, we shouldn't dismiss this story. People are paying scalper prices to attend a charismatic worship service where the preacher talks about hope and victory. That tells us untold numbers of people are lonely and hurting. They're longing to connect with a faith that binds their spiritual and emotional wounds. And it reminds us, as uncomfortable as we Baptists tend to be with it, that the Holy Spirit is powerful and at work among people who seek God.[104]

The Rise of Lakewood Church and Joel Osteen

This is the paradox of Joel Osteen's tour across America. "Religious" people seem to be very uncomfortable with Joel, his message, and the attention he attracts. They want to call his message "Christianity Lite," and yet his message speaks to the needs of thousands, if not millions, of people across the country. Lakewood's musicians win Dove Awards and sell millions of albums. Worship services fill arenas across the country with people who never sit in a pew. Much of the secular press is impressed by this young man, who seems so nice and is attracting the attention of thousands of people in large cities across America. They would like to find a way to label him, but he attracts crowds in red states as well as blue. He refuses to sit in judgment on anyone. They don't understand how people can fall for his religious line, but Joel Osteen seems harmless to them.

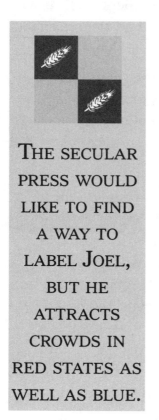

THE SECULAR PRESS WOULD LIKE TO FIND A WAY TO LABEL JOEL, BUT HE ATTRACTS CROWDS IN RED STATES AS WELL AS BLUE.

The largest one-night crowd for "An Evening with Joel Osteen" was at the Alamodome in San Antonio. Buses were chartered by Lakewood members to come up from Houston and support the cause. These members were some of the thirty-eight thousand people who worshiped there on May 13, 2005.

Joel and the team continued to minister across the country throughout the summer of 2005. In Philadelphia they worked with Larry Jones' Feed the Children and asked people to bring canned goods to their services. The food was to be distributed in the community where the service was being held. This quickly became a normal part of the events across the country.[105] The one blip occurred in the fall when they were scheduled to have a service in Birmingham, Alabama, which had to be cancelled due to Hurricane Katrina. By that time, Joel and the leadership team had turned their focus toward helping hurricane victims in the Gulf area, anyway.

In the year following the first event in Atlanta, hundreds of thousands of people in cities far from Houston were able to experience a Lakewood service in person. They were able to praise the Lord and dance in the aisles with Cindy and the Lakewood orchestra. They were able to hear Dodie, Victoria, Paul, and sometimes Lisa tell stories about the family and how God had been faithful for these many years. They got to hear Joel talk about how we are to be victors and not victims. They were able to be among the thousands of people who, when Joel asked the question, stood to indicate they wanted to give their lives to the Lord. They repeated a prayer of salvation and received material from Lakewood encouraging them to read the Bible and to get into a good church.

"An Evening with Joel Osteen" has become a regular part of the ministry of Joel Osteen and Lakewood Church. They continue to hold services in major cities every three or four weeks. In the fall of 2005, over fifty thousand people attended three services in the New York City area, one service on Long Island and two services in Madison Square Garden. The month before they went back to New York, Joel and the team ministered in Washington, D.C., truly the home of the nation's movers and shakers.

LAKEWOOD SATELLITES?

The events around the country may also be setting the stage for Lakewood Church to open satellite churches throughout the nation. Today many churches have started satellite churches at locations away from their main campuses. Second Baptist Church of Houston, one of the largest churches in the country at this writing, has five locations in the Houston area. Life Church in Oklahoma City is also one of the largest churches in the country and has several locations, including one in Arizona, a thousand miles away from the primary campus. In this day of high-speed Internet and video conferencing, it has become increasingly easier and affordable to conduct video services at any number of locations.

The question has to be asked: if Joel and the Lakewood team can attract thousands of people to sporting arenas around the country, how many people in those same cities would attend live worship services viewed on a large video screen? If even 10 percent of the people who attend "An Evening with Joel Osteen" would attend a live service viewed over a video screen, then Lakewood Church could grow by tens of thousands in weekly attendance within a very short time. Many of these people, who do not routinely go to church, must like the style of worship services conducted by Lakewood or they would not watch on TV or attend the events. They may well be hungry to be a part of that kind of worship experience on a regular basis.

Joel has said that he anticipates having one hundred thousand people worshiping weekly at Lakewood. Creating satellite services around the country could make this happen very quickly. In the two years since that first event in Atlanta, services have been conducted in over twenty cities. Averaging two thousand people in satellite services in these twenty cities alone would bring Lakewood up to nearly one hundred thousand people in weekly services. Change this number to five thousand and the total approaches one hundred fifty thousand people. People who receive Jesus as a result of the television program could be sent to local Lakewood congregations. When Joel does personal appearances at bookstores people could receive information regarding local Lakewood congregations. When events are held in sporting arenas, the attendees could be invited to local Lakewood congregations during the services. The potential impact of this is difficult to imagine. Joel and Lakewood would have a presence in many major cities overnight.

"An Evening with Joel Osteen" has been a stroke of genius for Lakewood Church over the last two years. It has brought Joel and Lakewood attention in communities all across the country. This has, in turn, provided publicity for Joel's books and for the television program. Indeed, the synergy of the Lakewood efforts is amazing. And it works! Everything benefits everything else. Time will tell if Lakewood decides to take this synergy and do something else with it in the communities where outreaches are held. Joel and the Lakewood staff have created a very big opportunity for themselves; it remains to be seen what they will do with it.

chapter nineteen

THE COMPAQ CENTER

Unless the LORD builds the house, they labor in vain who build it.
—Psalm 127:1

F our services each week were stretching Lakewood's facilities to the brink. The Saturday night service wasn't so bad, but back-to-back-to-back services on Sunday were taxing everyone's strength and endurance. On Sundays, the choir would sing at all three services, after having sung at the Saturday night service a few hours before. They would be at church for nearly eight hours on the weekend. Add to that all the hours put in by ushers, nursery workers, bookstore and information booth volunteers, parking lot attendants, and the vast number of people who make Lakewood the marvelous worship experience that it is.

When John was alive, he talked about building a twenty-five-thousand-seat auditorium at their East Houston location. John also spoke of moving to a larger location—The Summit, Houston's downtown sports arena, later renamed the Compaq Center. Studies were done to determine what would be the best solution. To expand the campus in East Houston would have required a great deal of cooperation from the city of Houston as well as the neighbors around the church. The city would have had to have helped them acquire the right-of-way to expand the road from Loop 610 from two lanes to four. This would have involved taking a major part of the front yards of many homes as well as displacing a number of families and local businesses. This would not have made Lakewood very popular with the neighborhood and would have created a public relations nightmare.

Even if the transportation problem could have been solved, building a new auditorium would have been a major undertaking. Thousands of additional parking spaces would have been needed. To avoid making people walk a half-mile or more to church would have required either a multistory parking garage or a commuter bus service to shuttle people from distant lots. Building a church auditorium seating fifteen to twenty thousand from the ground up would have been expensive. The new eighteen-thousand-seat arena that the Houston Rockets were building was going to cost them two hundred two million dollars.[106] Lakewood didn't need all the luxury suites and amenities, but the cost of quality sound as well as air conditioning for a building of this size would not be cheap. The final analysis was clear. It would be difficult if not impossible for Lakewood to expand at their East Houston location. Another solution had to be found.

So, Joel and his team began to look for suitable land to buy. Finding a hundred or more acres of undeveloped land close to a major highway is not a simple task. Then, when the land is found, determinations must be made as to whether the soil is suitable for the construction of a major building. The type of soil, drainage, and other environmental issues need to be considered. Skyline Wesleyan Church, in San Diego, had to work for nearly two decades to relocate their church campus.

It was not only a lengthy endeavor, but it was also a costly one. Nearly $27 million was spent constructing a $6 million building, due to environmental, topographical, and bureaucratic challenges.[107] Houston officials might have proved more receptive to a church relocating than were the officials in California, but that was not to say that it would be a simple move.

Several possibilities were investigated, but none of them seemed right. They attempted to purchase one hundred acres near the ship channel. They spent well into six figures on soil samples and environmental studies and signed a letter of intent, but when they went to sign sale papers, they found that the property had been sold the night before. Joel described it this way: "It was weird. The people just decided overnight not to sell [to Lakewood]. It was just the hand of God. Of course, at the time we thought it was the devil."

Finally, in the summer of 2000, it was announced that the Houston Rockets basketball team would be relocating their games to a new arena that was to be built. It was to be completed in time for the 2003–04 season. Immediately, Lakewood expressed interest in relocating to the Rockets's old home, the Compaq Center.

ROAD TO THE COMPAQ CENTER

The Compaq Center solved a number of problems. It had a seating capacity of nearly eighteen thousand. Changes would need to be made, but even with those changes, there would be enough seats to accommodate the growing congregation. In addition, there was obviously enough parking for the arena because thousands of cars already parked there for the games and concerts.

The Rise of Lakewood Church and Joel Osteen

The first public mention of Lakewood's interest in the Compaq Center was reported in the *Houston Chronicle* on October 29, 2000. The article said that Lakewood had a "keen interest" in the property. It also explained that the Compaq Center was landlocked by the Greenway Plaza, a business park development owned by Crescent Real Estate Equities, the company that controlled all the parking and air conditioning for the building.

THE PROPOSAL BETWEEN LAKEWOOD AND THE CITY WAS DESCRIBED AS A "WIN-WIN" SITUATION.

City councilman Mark Goldberg was quoted as saying, "Crescent absolutely must be able to dictate what happens to Compaq Center. Before anyone would lease or buy it, we have to deal with that issue." These words were to prove prophetic over the next several months. At that point Lakewood had not made a formal offer, but Goldberg predicted that it would take a million dollars or more a year to lease the building.[108]

By the spring of 2001, the city of Houston was formally taking offers for the facility. Prior to the city's request, the only proposals the city had received were from Lakewood and Grace Community Church. Both offers were to lease the property. At that point a thirty-year lease was being discussed with a possible option for an additional thirty years. But there was still an open acknowledgement that Crescent would have to be reckoned with due to the parking and air conditioning situations. Without Crescent, it was just a very hot building with no parking. There was another major issue as well. If someone leased the Compaq Center, no concerts or other events could be held there that would compete with the new arena being built for the Rockets. This severely limited other parties who might have been interested in the property.

In June 2001, it was announced that Lakewood had made a formal offer of 9.5 million dollars to lease the building for thirty years. The facility would be transformed into Lakewood International Center, with the church spending 69 million dollars on renovations, which included a seventy-five-hundred-vehicle parking facility and an upgraded air conditioning system. Jordy Tollett, director of the city's Convention and Entertainment Department, called the proposal a "win-win" situation.[109] Councilman Goldberg said that he had expected a million dollars a year, but that the proposed upgrades made the offer attractive. Both of these men would play crucial roles in deciding the issue of the Compaq Center and Lakewood Church over the next several months. Tollett was also the mayor's chief of staff, and the Compaq Center was located in Goldberg's district. Their input and opinions would prove to be vital to Lakewood. Crescent Real Estate Equities had also made an offer, but no details were given.

Within a few days, the contest between Crescent and Lakewood became very public. A citizen's committee was appointed to look at the competing offers and they recommended Lakewood. The Lakewood offer was all cash. Additionally, Lakewood would make improvements to the facility and then hand the building back to the city after thirty years. Lakewood also agreed to spend 3.3 million a year on community outreach programs such as job training, health programs, and some Christian missionary services. They also agreed to allow the city to use the facility up to ten days a year for community events.

The offer from Crescent was much more complex. It involved a land swap with some other property they owned in the downtown area as well as two million dollars in debt forgiveness from the city regarding an old hotel deal that didn't work out. They also wanted permission to demolish the Compaq Center if they could not lease it within a year.[110]

Lakewood hired well-connected lobbyist Dave Walden, right-hand man of former mayor Bob Lanier, to assist them in their efforts to obtain the Compaq Center. There was some criticism of this because he was known as a chain-smoking, swearing, non-churchgoing, deal-making individual who was not known for embracing Christian values. This hire was done at the encouragement of Lakewood's attorneys to negotiate the lease with the city. When Joel was asked about his influence in the politics of Houston and what role he wanted to play, he insisted that he had no desire to become involved at any level in politics. Walden defended Joel, saying that he was telling the truth, calling him more of a "visionary" than a "wheeler-dealer." Walden said, "Anytime I get a client who really listens to me and doesn't try to do my job, they're worth their weight in gold. That's kinda how he was. You know, I was afraid to smoke in front of him, yeah. Only one time did I say a cuss word around him. Let me tell you, I'd run through a wall for the guy."

A vote was scheduled to determine which offer to accept and to begin the process of negotiations. It was postponed a week because of the absence of some council members, and this just served to increase the tension in the situation. The issue was on the agenda at the city council's July 3, 2001, meeting. It was clear early on that Lakewood had wide support from the council. Councilman and mayoral candidate Orlando Sanchez was to give the prayer opening the meeting. Instead he asked Joel to do the honors. The vote was made, and the city agreed to begin negotiations with Lakewood for a lease for the Compaq Center.[111] Crescent was not happy with the decision, and they had not yet given up the contest.

Shortly after the vote by the city council, Crescent Real Estate Equities filed a lawsuit to block the city from leasing the Compaq Center to Lakewood, claiming that the lease would violate a sixty-year-old deed restriction. The city countered with a motion to dismiss on the grounds there was no lease in place; therefore there was nothing to contest. In November the motion was heard and a federal judge agreed with the city.[112] The negotiations had been completed, and the city was due to consider the lease agreement shortly after the judge dismissed the motion. But Crescent had not yet thrown in the towel.

During the summer and fall, as negotiations were going on between the city and Lakewood, the city hired three different appraisers to establish a value for the Compaq Center. They set the value between 9.9 and 11.3 million dollars. But they also said that without air conditioning and parking, the value of the building would be negligible. They said the property would then be worth more if the arena were torn down and the land redeveloped into a mix of business and retail.[113]

On Wednesday, December 19, 2001, the Houston city council voted to lease the Compaq Center to Lakewood.[114] The agreement required a minimum of ten council members to vote in favor. As late as Monday there was doubt as to whether there were ten votes in the affirmative. Councilman Goldberg announced that he would offer some amendments to the proposal to charge Lakewood rent during the second thirty years of the lease and boost the amount of rent the church would pay during the first three years. With those changes he would vote to approve. Under the terms of the lease, the church would pay 9.5 million dollars for the first thirty years and get a second thirty years as long as they completed a minimum of 69 million dollars worth of improvements including a parking garage and air conditioning system. Crescent announced that as soon as the lease was approved they would refile their lawsuit.

In the final agreement, Lakewood agreed to pay 12.1 million for the first thirty years and 22.6 million for the second thirty years. They agreed to pay one million dollars a year for the first three years. In addition, the city of Houston was bidding for the 2012 Olympics at that time and Lakewood agreed that if the city were selected to host the Olympics, the building would be made available.[115] This later became moot when the city lost its bid. It was official; Lakewood would take possession in late 2003, when the new basketball arena was completed.

That Wednesday night, back at the church in East Houston, Joel and the congregation celebrated the vote. Although there had been some questions right up to the end, they had had faith that things would work out their way.

A Test of Joel's Leadership

This was the biggest challenge that Joel had faced in his short time as senior pastor. It had been over a year since they had first begun the process. Joel said it cost the church over a million dollars for lawyers, lobbyists, site studies, and other things necessary to make the deal happen.[116] But in the end it did happen. When Joel became senior pastor, he was the leader of the congregation in title and appearance. With the approval of the lease for the Compaq Center, he became the leader of the congregation in every sense of the term. Many at Lakewood have strong memories of John, and always will. But it was Joel who led them to become the largest church in America and Joel who led them to obtain the largest church sanctuary in America. Lakewood was no longer his daddy's church.

True to its word, Crescent filed a lawsuit in June of the following year, seeking to block the lease. In the suit they alleged that the lease violated the deed restrictions, which they said prohibited the land from being used for any purpose other than a commercial one. The city countered that nothing in the deed restrictions prohibited religious events. Indeed, the city said that over the years the Compaq Center had been leased for religious events on many occasions.[117]

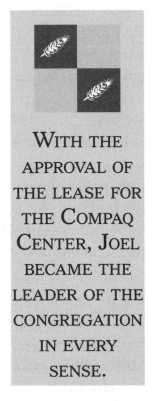

WITH THE APPROVAL OF THE LEASE FOR THE COMPAQ CENTER, JOEL BECAME THE LEADER OF THE CONGREGATION IN EVERY SENSE.

Finally, in December 2002, the situation with Crescent, Lakewood, and the city of Houston was settled. Lakewood agreed to pay 11.8 million dollars of its lease for the Compaq Center in "accelerated rent." The city would use the money to purchase some of Crescent's property near the Compaq Center. The city would also complete the purchase of Crescent's property with some additional funds obtained through other means. Crescent would drop the lawsuit and its opposition to Lakewood's lease. They also agreed to negotiate in good faith with Lakewood regarding parking around the Compaq Center.[118]

AN ARENA BECOMES A CHURCH

Joel and the Lakewood leadership team had already started preparing for the time when the Compaq Center would be theirs. When the proposal was made to the Houston city council for Lakewood to lease the Compaq Center, they had announced they would spend sixty-nine million dollars on renovations in the arena. As time went on, this number would change several times. But whatever the final number, they knew that renovating a sports arena into a worship center would not be inexpensive. They began the process of raising the funds for the renovations. They hired John Maxwell's organization, Injoy Stewardship Solutions, to assist them in raising the funds.

Joel spoke highly of Maxwell and his organization: "We knew raising the capital funds for this project would be a huge challenge, so we knew that it would be wise to enlist the finest consultants in this field. That's why we turned to John Maxwell and ISS to partner with us in meeting this need. It was absolutely, positively a powerful combination."[119]

Lakewood began the fund-raising process by asking people to sponsor a seat for the new building at a cost of twenty-five hundred dollars. They promised to place the name of everyone who sponsored a seat on a plaque in the new building. This was a three-year fund-raising campaign called Champion's Legacy. They established a special website where people could find information regarding the building's acquisition and renovation. Letters were mailed

to supporters of the church including the active membership in the Houston area and people who actively gave to
the television ministry. There was an immediate response
to the appeal.[120]

People like to be a part of something that captures the
imagination. They like to know that they are making a difference in some way with their lives and with their money.
Being a part of the largest church in
America is something that captures
the heart. Whether the church world
likes it or not, people are attracted to
Lakewood because Joel says that God
is a great God who wants to help His
people to succeed at life, and expects
us to live lives of integrity and accountability. This message and the success of
Lakewood have created an image across
America that has captured the hearts of
millions of people.

**OBTAINING
THE COMPAQ
CENTER SET
JOEL AND
LAKEWOOD
APART FROM
EVERY OTHER
PASTOR AND
CHURCH IN
AMERICA.**

Joel and the leadership team of
Lakewood understood that they needed
to do something with this opportunity
to make a difference. They were not
building the church sanctuary of their
parents or grandparents. It was bigger
and greater than anything they could have imagined. Sports
writers have often called new and elaborate sporting arenas
"cathedrals." Lakewood was preparing the place that would
be the cathedral of twenty-first-century Christians.

It was five years from the time Joel and Lakewood began
to pursue the Compaq Center until they held their first service

there. Along the way, Lakewood was required to borrow millions of dollars for the first time. Joel's father was well-known for completing all of Lakewood's buildings debt-free, with cash on hand. This established Joel as his own man, but it also placed a large target squarely on his back if things were to fail. But Joel recognized that they had only one opportunity to obtain a facility that would provide a worship center for the largest church in America on one of the busiest highways in America. Joel knew that it was the perfect place for Lakewood, and he never wavered. Obtaining the Compaq Center set Lakewood and Joel apart from every other church and pastor in America. While the spotlight had been strong before, it was even stronger now.

A New Home for Lakewood

On December 1, 2003, Mayor Lee Brown of Houston presented a key to Joel and Victoria Osteen, symbolizing possession of the former Compaq Center. There were about one hundred twenty people from Lakewood present for the presentation. Mayor Brown called it a new era for the Compaq Center. Joel said it was a dream come true. He announced that Lakewood would be building a five-story building on the Edloe Street side of the building to house programs for children, teens, and adults, as well as a broadcast center. The skyboxes would become offices and the former locker rooms would become nurseries.[121]

The groundbreaking services, which were held on December 13 and 14, captured the attention of Houston and the Christian world. It was as if nothing had been real until they actually held some kind of service in the building. It had been a long time coming for the people of Lakewood. It had been three-and-a-half years since the beginning of the process of obtaining use of the arena. It had taken a year and a half for the council to vote for Lakewood to be awarded the lease. There had been another two years while the new arena for the Houston Rockets was completed. In the meantime there were lawsuits and other obstacles to overcome.

The staff spent the two weeks between the key ceremony and the groundbreaking service preparing the arena for the weekend celebration services. A temporary stage was built and large screens were set in place so that everyone could see what was taking place on stage. A large combined choir, who were to wear shirts of the same color, prepared to lift up praises. A makeshift sound system had to be set up so that everyone could hear the music and the message.

The Saturday night service was packed. Joel told the crowd, "We're gonna totally change the look of the place and build out children's facilities, new sound and lighting, and change the floor, so it's not going to look like the same."[122] At the end of the service, the Lakewood leadership team, including the entire Osteen family, as well as some public officials, came to the stage, took shovels, and dug into a trough of dirt. The audience broke into cheers.

The transformation of the Compaq Center began almost immediately after the groundbreaking weekend. By the time they were able to take possession of the building, much of the preliminary work had already been done, so they were able to move relatively quickly once they had access and permission to start the process. But renovating an arena and building a five-story building cannot be done overnight, no matter how much the process is rushed.

chapter twenty

OCCUPYING THE
PROMISED LAND

I will bring you into the land which I swore to give to
Abraham, Isaac, and Jacob; and I will give it to you
as a heritage: I am the LORD.
—Exodus 6:8

Entering any promised land starts long before you ever set one foot in the land. Joel Osteen's promised land was not one of milk and honey, but an eighteen-thousand-seat sports arena. When the city council initially voted to approve Lakewood's proposal to lease the facility, it was published that Lakewood would move into its new home at the end of 2003. That date was delayed several times. When Lakewood finally obtained the lease, it announced that they would complete renovations in twelve months. Lakewood officials were confident that all the work could be done within a year.[123] They had been working for some time to prepare so that they could hit the ground running once they had possession. One of the single biggest expenditures they knew they would have was the cost of air conditioning—a cool twenty million dollars.

Work began almost immediately after the celebration service in December 2003. In addition to doing a makeover of the arena, Lakewood planned a five-story building annexed to the arena that would house the programs for children, youth, and adults, plus a state-of-the-art broadcast production center. The church would also add to the complex a wedding chapel, conference rooms, a bookstore, and a food court.

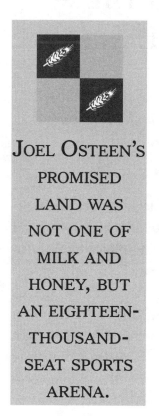

JOEL OSTEEN'S PROMISED LAND WAS NOT ONE OF MILK AND HONEY, BUT AN EIGHTEEN-THOUSAND-SEAT SPORTS ARENA.

It was soon determined that the actual length of time needed to complete the project would be two years. Very early in the process, the decision was made to shorten the period to eighteen months. To meet the challenge, they would split the project construction documents into twenty-two separate drawing projects to be released over a period of ten months. Each document package had a budget assigned to it and was bid on separately by all the contractors. Every effort was made to hold costs down by retaining anything in the arena that could be used in the new worship center. In the end, thirteen of the basketball arena's eighteen thousand seats were used in the worship center, with three thousand new seats installed.[124]

As the date of completion drew near, church members were invited to go to the Compaq Center and lay a spiritual foundation for the "new land." Members were encouraged to sign their names, write Bible verses, or put other greetings on the walls and floors before they were painted or covered with carpet or tile. A special time was reserved for "invitation only" guests.

Each of these invited guests also received an autographed copy of Joel's book; many of these books also included a written note of encouragement from Joel's son, Jonathan. It was a way to thank all those who had committed to "buy a seat" at the new facility and to encourage them to continue with their weekly or monthly giving.

Completing projects like this always requires a dance of sorts between the owner and his contractor. Building contractors like to have as much time as possible to complete the project, and owners want to move in and get started. This takes lots of planning and clear communication, with as much lead time as possible. Joel and his project managers had to sit down with the contractors to determine exactly when the projected date of completion could be. Once the date was announced, the contractors would be committed to doing everything possible to achieve construction completion by that date. The contractors wanted the grand opening to be in September, but Joel and the church leadership wanted the date to be as soon as July. Compromises and promises were made. Crews would be scheduled around the clock. But the word went out to everyone that Lakewood would be moving to its new location on the weekend of July 16 and 17.[125]

Eleven weeks out, the countdown began in the weekend bulletin. Billboards began to spring up all over Houston inviting people to be a part of the new home. Every Lakewood television program contained an announcement about the big day. There would be a video invitation at the beginning and end of each program, with an announcer inviting the viewers to come and be a part of the special day. Joel and his team understood marketing very well and wanted to make the most of this event. They knew there had to be a flood of publicity preceding it.

Joel believed that with the move to the former Compaq Center, Lakewood would soon be hosting over one hundred thousand worshipers each weekend.[126] It takes an army of volunteers to assist that many people in having a worship experience. In the weeks before move-in Sunday, a wide appeal was made for additional volunteers. At the east Houston location, it took about twelve hundred volunteers to conduct services. Now there would be a need for three thousand volunteers each Sunday. That was nearly a 300 percent increase in volunteer support. These new volunteers would need to be trained, badges had to be created, and an organizational structure had to be set in place so that all would know where they were supposed to be and when.

The campaign to attract volunteers was called "Living the Life." Notices in the weekly bulletin and video announcements encouraged people to become involved and indicated that their lives would be strengthened through serving. Volunteers needed to submit to background checks and had to have attended Lakewood Church for at least three months.

During the weeks and months before the opening, sneak previews were given by Joel personally to some of the local media. They were able to take pictures of the new facility and report on all the changes that Lakewood had made to one of the most familiar spots in Houston. In the days before the big weekend, the media, as well as some of the volunteers, came into the building to look around and prepare for the guests who would be attending. What they saw was that the basketball court was gone. The main stage had been placed at one end, and the floor was sloped to be more like a theater than an arena. Lighting was used to place the focus on the stage instead of the center court. The media also inspected the new five-story building built along Edloe Street. When the media reported about their tour of the facility, they also reported on available parking, which provided another avenue to get the word out to people about the weekend services. Everything was in place for one of the greatest weekends in American church history.

Interested people all over the world were able to view the progress of construction through cameras that broadcasted directly onto Lakewood's website. Joel and his staff were aware of the importance of communication in raising funds. Progress reports were made in services as well as through the local media. Videos were used in services to show the progress of the construction of the five-story building, as well as the work on the arena. The fact that the facility was located at the second busiest corner in America meant that hundreds of thousands of motorists were aware of the progress by personally viewing it each day.

THIS ONETIME SPORTING ARENA HAD BEEN TRANSFORMED INTO A BEAUTIFUL PLACE OF WORSHIP.

Finally the big July weekend arrived. The very first service was scheduled for seven o'clock on Saturday evening. By six o'clock, traffic had slowed to a crawl a mile away from the church. Those caught in the traffic jam noticed that people were already walking away from the church. Police officers every hundred yards or so informed everyone that the church was full. No one else would be allowed to enter the building; no seats were available. Not only were there no seats available, but there was also nowhere to park outside. Amazingly, a church with access to 8,500 parking spaces had run out of parking. Ushers handed out bulletins to those who still wanted a souvenir to show that they had attempted to attend the service.

Inside the church, those lucky enough to arrive early saw that this onetime sporting arena had been magnificently transformed into a beautiful place of worship. Everything seemed to be floating in a sea of sky blue beams of light flowing from the ceiling to the floor. Heavenly clouds appeared to be suspended behind the choir. The drapes behind the band, the walls, and the giant spinning globe all reflected the creative lighting effects on stage. Even the band's music stands were continually changing images and color designs. Joel and the Lakewood team knew that effective lighting would help set the mood for everything that was going to happen. It helped to establish a feeling of intimacy, even in a venue as large as Lakewood.

The new home of Lakewood was designed for one thing and one thing alone: leading people to the throne of God. The pulpit was framed by beautiful waterfalls and backed by a large globe of the world. Everything was bathed in light that allowed everyone to easily focus on whatever was happening onstage. High above the floor, the ceiling was laced with a series of catwalks, but above the catwalks was a ceiling with beautiful colors that changed from time to time. Duncan Dodds told the *New York Times* that their goal was to appeal to all the senses and take your breath away.[127]

The excited crowd reflected the diversity that had always been a part of Lakewood. The variety of races and ethnic backgrounds were fully at ease sitting next to and conversing with each other. Of course many VIPs were in attendance as well. Governor Rick Perry said to the reporters attending, "It is so great to look across a crowd and see the wonderful diversity of this great state we call Texas. As lawmakers we do a lot of things, but only the church can teach people to love."[128] House minority leader Nancy Pelosi and other members of Congress were present as well as the Houston city council, and other Texas and U.S. politicians.

As I wrote earlier, the service itself was as much a tribute to the past as it was a celebration of the present. The service featured videos that illustrated various points in the history of Lakewood: John and the beginning of Lakewood; the transition from East Houston to the Compaq Center; and all that was done to make the move to the Compaq Center.

Paul Osteen continued the tribute with the help of the Osteen grandchildren. In a touching presentation, Paul introduced various items called "stones" that had helped to mark the path of Lakewood. He brought out one of his dad's Bibles, a chair from the original feed store, a pair of his dad's shoes, one of the bumper stickers found on the backs of cars all over Houston, a chair from the East Houston location, a brochure from when Joel became pastor, and the symbolic key to the former Compaq Center.

Except for the fact that it was the first service in the new building, Lakewood did nothing special for the weekend. Lakewood was just having church. There were no special speakers, no special singers, and nothing else was different from what they do at Lakewood every weekend. Foregoing the temptation to bring in a special speaker for the occasion— a nationally known evangelist, a prominent Christian writer, a public figure, or a politician—Lakewood opted to keep the main thing the main thing. They realized that with fifty thousand or more people present that weekend, hundreds if not thousands would need to accept Jesus Christ as their Savior. This was a great opportunity to bring the gospel to people who needed to hear it. Joel spoke about making dreams come true and shared that just as God had made the dream of acquiring the former Compaq Center come true for Lakewood, He could and would make our dreams come true as well.

At the end of the service, Joel asked people to stand if they wanted to receive Christ as Savior. There was really no way to get an accurate count, but hundreds of people stood all over the auditorium.

On Sunday, crowd management continued to be a challenge as fourteen thousand people tried to leave the first service at the same time that nearly sixteen thousand were trying to get in. Where once a crowd of eighteen thousand was considered a full house, now there were thirty thousand people in the same space trying to move around. Outside there were parking problems. People coming in could not find a parking place because the people inside had not left yet. Inside, particularly around the entrance doors to the auditorium, there was no space for anyone to move.

Later it was reported that 57,000 people attended the services that weekend. No church in America has ever had such a weekend. Back in the 1970s, the First Baptist Church of Hammond, Indiana, gave an account of having had over one hundred thousand people on one weekend. It was done with a large bus ministry and services held in neighborhoods all over the Chicagoland area. The vast majority of those attending were children. At that time, First Baptist was the largest church in the country, with twenty thousand on average in weekly attendance, half of that number being children, who arrived in Sunday school buses. But within a twenty-four-hour period, no church in the United States had ever had so many adults come to worship services at one location as during the opening weekend of Lakewood's new facilities. The former Compaq Center, with the children's facilities and nurseries, gives Lakewood the capability to minister to twenty thousand adults, teens, and children at a time. Presently they have four services each weekend, giving them an immediate potential capacity of eighty thousand people!

During the opening weekend, they discovered several details of a practical manner that needed to be completed. For example, there were no paper towel holders in the men's room. The lack of maneuvering space for the crowds between the two English services had to be dealt with. But most of these problems were really organizational and could be addressed when wise people put their minds together.

THE REAL CHALLENGE WAS DEVELOPING OPPORTUNITIES FOR SPIRITUAL MATURITY FOR SUCH A LARGE GATHERING OF PEOPLE EACH WEEK.

The real challenge was developing opportunities for spiritual maturity for such a large gathering of people each week. One of the real complaints about megachurches is that people can come and go and never be noticed. If someone can come in and out of a church of two to five thousand, then coming in and out of a church of eighty thousand is even easier. Disicpleship in this context is one of the greatest responsibilities that can be imagined. God will hold the leaders of Lakewood responsible for this. To show they were to the task, Lakewood needed to develop classes and fellowship opportunities so that people could grow in the Lord.

When John was alive and pastoring Lakewood, he made certain people grew spiritually from the milk to the meat of the Word. This is the spiritual foundation that has allowed Lakewood to achieve all they have achieved today. For Joel and the Lakewood leadership team to take the church to a higher level still, they will need to demonstrate that they can take thousands of people to a higher level spiritually. Joel and his father, John, can be compared to Joshua and his father in the ministry, Moses. Moses and John both led the people to a promised land but did not get to enter themselves. Joshua and Joel both stepped into the land with the people. The job before Joel now: just what will he do in the promised land?

chapter twenty-one

LAKEWOOD: THE LARGEST CHURCH IN AMERICA

Many people shall come and say, "Come, and let us go up to the mountain of the LORD, to the house of the God of Jacob; He will teach us His ways, and we shall walk in His paths."
—Isaiah 2:3

I n interviews and reports of the opening weekend, Lakewood was compared to Roger Banister, the man who first broke the four-minute mile. Within months after he broke this record, which many thought could never be done, the same record was broken by many people. It was now suggested that Lakewood was setting a mark for churches all over the country. Now that one church had moved into an arena averaging fifty thousand or more in weekly attendance, the bar would be raised for other churches as well.

In 1969, Dr. Elmer Towns wrote a book about the ten largest Sunday schools in America. The largest church at that time was Akron Baptist Temple, averaging 5,762 weekly in Sunday school. At that time, eight of the ten largest churches were independent Baptist, one was Southern Baptist, and the other was independent charismatic. The tenth largest Sunday school was listed with an attendance of 2,453.[129] Twenty-four years later, Dr. John N. Vaughan wrote a book entitled, *Megachurches*

The Rise of Lakewood Church and Joel Osteen

& *America's Cities.* In his list of the top ten, the leading church was still independent Baptist, First Baptist Church of Hammond, Indiana, averaging twenty thousand. But four of the top ten churches were now averaging over ten thousand; only one was Baptist, and it was Southern Baptist. The tenth largest church listed had an attendance of eight thousand.[130] In 2005, *Outreach* magazine, with the assistance of Dr. Vaughan, listed the top one hundred largest and fastest-growing churches in America. Lakewood was listed as the largest with an average weekly attendance of 32,500, but even the lowest of the top ten had an average weekly attendance of 18,420.

Where once the bar was five thousand in weekly attendance, the number is now eighty thousand. In the last decade, any one of a dozen churches has been called the largest in America. Willow Creek in the Chicago area has been widely reported to be the largest. Saddleback Church in Southern California has also been called the largest. At times, Phoenix First Assembly and Calvary Chapel in Santa Anna have been given the title. Today, Lakewood not only has undisputed claim to the title of largest church in America, but they are also almost twice the size of the second largest church. On any given Sunday, several churches have a chance to be the second largest church in America, but only one church will be the largest for the next year or two. If a church is going to surpass Lakewood, it has a lot of work to do.

There are many who would be uncomfortable with this kind of attendance contest. Of course, there isn't a real contest in the ordinary sense of the term. But, when specific churches excel in reaching their cities for Christ, it does draw attention. When the churches are similar in doctrine or traditions to some other churches, it challenges the others within those doctrines or traditions to stretch themselves and try to do more to reach people.

Some pastors will share information on techniques or methods that were successful in their area. Today there are five Southern Baptist churches in the top fifteen. Two of them have a father and son for pastors. Second Baptist Church of Houston and Fellowship Church in Grapevine, Texas, each have a pastor named Ed Young. Ed Young Sr. is in Houston, and Ed Young Jr. is in the Dallas area. In addition, Ed Young Jr. has written a book with Andy Stanley of the Atlanta area, who is also the son of well-known pastor Charles Stanley. These pastors challenge each other to examine their methods and techniques to reach their cities for Jesus. They attend and speak at conferences all over the country and host conferences at their churches where they share the methods and tools they have used with other Southern Baptists and with others of similar evangelical non-charismatic traditions.

Today, Lakewood Church is almost twice the size of the second-largest church in America.

There are also a number of Pentecostal or charismatic churches in the 2005 top fifteen. In addition to Lakewood, there are also three African-American charismatic churches: Potter's House with Bishop T. D. Jakes in the Dallas area; and New Birth Missionary Baptist Church with Bishop Eddie Long in Atlanta; and World Changers Church International with Pastor Creflo Dollar, also in Atlanta. There is also Calvary Chapel Church in Fort Lauderdale, which is the largest of a number of Calvary Chapel megachurches around the country. First Assembly in Phoenix with Pastor Tommy Barnett is the largest of the Assemblies of God churches in the country.

The final group of churches near the top are the independent, evangelical, non-charismatic churches. Among them are Willow Creek Community Church, in the Chicago area, and Southeast Christian Church, in Louisville. These two churches and others like them are prominently featured in such evangelical publications as *Christianity Today* and its sister publication, *Leadership Journal*. Their pastors and ministry leaders have published articles describing the methods and techniques they have used to reach their cities for Jesus.

These churches are not in competition with each other, but they do establish the standard for each other, as well as for the churches within their denominations, fellowships, or spheres of influence. They share methods and techniques that have been used successfully, and some that have not been so successful.

America is no longer the "mom-and-pop" place it was in the 1950s. The methods of the 1950s will not work in the twenty-first century. There are many venues that compete for the attention of people today. There are hundreds of channels on the television, including a variety of Christian networks. There are millions of options on the Internet, with many Christian outlets there as well. To act as though there is no competition for the attention of people is foolish. The question is, how are the churches of the twenty-first century going to compete? We will learn from those who are successfully reaching their cities with methods and techniques that fit within the religious traditions we espouse. We will learn by watching those who are making a difference. Does this mean there will be thousands of megachurches all over the country? Yes and no. There will be more megachurches than ever before, but there will also be thousands of churches who have learned to make a difference in their communities by reaching a few hundred people, not thousands.

We are already seeing some of this come to pass. As I mentioned previously, we are also seeing megachurches operate from multiple locations. Technology now allows a church to send a live feed of any or all of its service to another location. This location could be a few miles or thousands of miles away. To many traditionalists, this may seem strange, but when you visit these churches, they seem vibrant and very normal. The gathering of hundreds of people all around you provides the feeling of being at church. These churches will seek out a few volunteer families to pioneer a new location, while providing basic services like children's ministries and greeters. Often, these satellite churches will grow to several hundred within a few months. The option for satellite campuses using low-cost video technology has only been available for a few years. There is no reason this technology could not be used to plant churches anywhere in the world. Language would be the only barrier; to overcome. Undoubtedly, there will be other innovations in the very near future that could be used to expand the reach of churches with a desire to win the world.

When asked about the future, Joel says he doesn't know what the future holds, but he also says that when a church consistently reaches 80 percent capacity, it has to seek larger facilities or add another service. He has openly discussed reaching one hundred thousand people a week at Lakewood. He jokes about Reliant Stadium, but who knows what is in the back of his mind? Duncan Dodds spoke of the possibility of satellite locations for Lakewood. He said, "I can't speak for pastor [Joel], but I can see us having Lakewood Philadelphia, Lakewood Atlanta, Lakewood Detroit, and having Joel preach the message every week. I think we could have churches of four thousand to six thousand. I see the potential there from a marketing side, I see the opportunity to expand this ministry and almost franchise it in that way. I think we will get there."[131] In a recent interview it was revealed that plans are underway for taking "An Evening with Joel Osteen" to Europe and Australia. If Lakewood can attract an arena full of people overseas, how much more difficult would it be to have services overseas on a regular basis through video?

This is an obvious fit considering Lakewood's abilities in broadcasting and video. Again, at the present time, all of the Lakewood services are webcast live over the internet. To send that signal with a little higher quality to remote locations would take very little effort or money. The question remains, how many people would come to a central location each week to be a part of a service where Joel Osteen spoke on a video screen?

Where are Joel Osteen and Lakewood Church going from here? No one knows. But this one thing is certain: Joel and his staff will not sit still. They will strive to do whatever they can to make a difference and touch this nation and the world for Jesus Christ.

chapter twenty-two

CRITICISMS AND CONCERNS

Blessed are you when they revile and persecute you, and say all kinds of evil against you falsely for My sake. Rejoice and be exceedingly glad, for great is your reward in heaven, for so they persecuted the prophets who were before you.
—Matthew 5:11–12

J oel Osteen is pastor of the largest church in America. He is a best-selling author who just signed a lucrative contract for his second major book. He leads a television ministry that is, by most surveys, the most watched Christian television show in the world. He fills sporting arenas around the country. People stand in long lines to get an autograph on a book, or a short personal word of prayer, or just to see that famous smile in person. Joel Osteen exists in rarified air indeed. But, of course, none of this comes without drawing a fair amount of critics and detractors.

There are those who observe the situation at Lakewood with a degree of skepticism, and sometimes with pronouncements of heresy. Some of the criticisms are from those with honest disagreements rooted in theological differences and conflicting traditions. Some are from right-wing, ultra-conservative groups who have no sympathies with anyone who reads from anything other than the King James Version of the Bible. Others are part of a group that is new to the Christian world—bloggers. There are hundreds of blogs on the Internet dedicated to pastors in America who appear to be doing something for the kingdom of God. Sometimes these blogs become valid means of discussion where the pros and cons of the issues are fairly discussed. Most of the time, however, they are biased efforts to anonymously smear the hard work of good people.

A Lack of Qualifications

When John Osteen died, there was a great deal of speculation about who would be his successor. One of the local television stations openly said that one of the worst things Lakewood could do would be to choose a member of the Osteen family to succeed him. There was some logic behind this reasoning because Paul was a surgeon in Little Rock and Joel had only preached once before his father's death. Gary Simon was youth pastor and worship leader, but he had no experience being the senior pastor of megachurch and certainly would not have been a guaranteed success. In both the print and electronic media, it was predicted that Lakewood would very likely choose an outsider as successor. This was the scenario in which Joel Osteen became senior pastor of Lakewood Church.

It was widely proclaimed in some areas of the media that Joel was a bad choice due to his lack of training, education, and experience. He had dropped out of Oral Roberts University after only one year. He had never served in any type of pastoral capacity at any church in his life. He had never preached until the Sunday before his father's death. Even then,

Joel himself called it a miracle that he was preaching and said that the congregation should remember this moment because it probably would never happen again. Although he did preach thirty-three of the thirty-six weeks between the death of John and his designation as senior pastor, that could hardly be called a great deal of experience. But only God could see the entire picture, and it would take time for Joel to see it clearly.

It is true that Joel was inexperienced and lacks formal training. But, again, one big area of training that Joel did receive was the seventeen years he spent ministering with his father. During that time, Joel not only heard his father speak every Sunday, but he also dissected the sermons each week as he edited them into a twenty-six-minute message for television. Each sermon was analyzed to make certain that all of the meat was in the program. This was a course in homiletics that very few Bible colleges or seminaries could match.

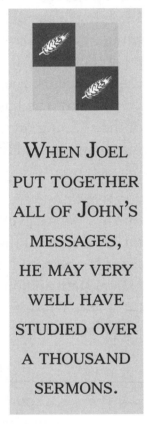

WHEN JOEL PUT TOGETHER ALL OF JOHN'S MESSAGES, HE MAY VERY WELL HAVE STUDIED OVER A THOUSAND SERMONS.

In addition to the weekly messages, Joel accompanied his father as he preached in villages and cities around the world. There can be little doubt that when Joel put together all these messages, he may very well have studied over a thousand sermons.

Learning to lead a megachurch is different from pastoring a normal suburban church. The senior pastor of a megachurch is more like the CEO of a major corporation, with the responsibility of a major budget and oversight of the spiritual care of thousands of people. The senior pastor of a megachurch must be as adept at handling administrative and management issues as he is in knowledge of the Bible and doctrine. Learning to pastor a megachurch like Lakewood is not something any Bible college or seminary can effectively prepare its students for. If you study megachurches established in the last twenty years or so, there is a pattern to the type of young man who has become pastor of these churches. Many of these young men have been mentored by pastors of other megachurches. Many of them have served on the staff of a megachurch.

Working every day with his father gave Joel an insight that few people ever obtain without actually being senior pastor. He learned skills by watching his father do the task every day. He observed his father as he interacted with his congregation, staff, and other people both in the church and around the world. This informal mentorship allowed Joel to develop a vision for Lakewood Church.

JOEL'S DOCTRINE

There are some critics who have raised issues about the style of messages that Joel brings to the congregation of Lakewood. As mentioned earlier, *Christianity Today's* 2005 review of Joel's book placed a lot of emphasis upon Joel's positive spin on Christianity and his prosperity theology.[132]

The issue of positive theology is one that creates a major chasm between evangelicals on one side, and charismatics and Pentecostals on the other. Some critics on the Internet refer to Joel as "Prosperity's Coverboy." Yet, many nationally known evangelists and pastors have embraced similar teachings for years, including men like Oral Roberts, Kenneth Hagin, Kenneth Copeland, Benny Hinn, T. D. Jakes, and, of course, John Osteen. The doctrine is built on a number of passages of Scripture. One of the best known is Luke 6:38:

> *Give, and it will be given to you; good measure, pressed down, shaken together, running over, they will pour into your lap.* (Luke 6:38 NASB)

Another passage often quoted is:

> *Remember this: Whoever sows sparingly will also reap sparingly, and whoever sows generously will also reap generously. Each man should give what he has decided in his heart to give, not reluctantly or under compulsion, for God loves a cheerful giver. And God is able to make all grace abound to you, so that in all things at all times, having all that you need, you will abound in every good work. As it is written: "He has scattered abroad his gifts to the poor; his righteousness endures forever." Now he who supplies seed to the sower and bread for food will also supply and increase your store of seed and will enlarge the harvest of your righteousness. You will be made rich in every way so that you can be generous on every occasion, and through us your generosity will result in thanksgiving to God.* (2 Corinthians 9:6–11 NIV)

The book of Proverbs has similar passages:

> *One man gives freely, yet gains even more; another withholds unduly, but comes to poverty. A generous man will prosper; he who refreshes others will himself be refreshed.* (Proverbs 11:24–25 NIV)

The Rise of Lakewood Church and Joel Osteen

He who is kind to the poor lends to the LORD, and he will reward him for what he has done. (Proverbs 19:17 NIV)

Those who disagree argue that if God blesses those who are faithful, then why are there millions of Christians around the world who struggle to meet their basic needs? These people will tend to place an emphasis upon eternal rewards, with no expectation of earthly ones. For centuries, churches have encouraged people to be complacent in their lives, looking forward to heaven and, therefore, willing to tolerate anything on earth. For such churches, telling parishioners that God desired to bless them would not preserve the status quo among the people. It would only encourage people to reach out and try to attempt to do more in God's name. It would encourage them to have hope and believe that they were special in the eyes of God because they were faithful to Him in their giving and living. In the end, this would make the people much harder to control and subdue.

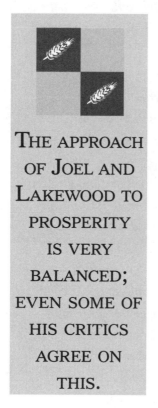

THE APPROACH OF JOEL AND LAKEWOOD TO PROSPERITY IS VERY BALANCED; EVEN SOME OF HIS CRITICS AGREE ON THIS.

The issue here is as much the culture and doctrine of evangelical churches across America as it is the prosperity gospel. One church teaches tithing and says that tithing will cause God to bless us, but doesn't give any real definition as to what the blessing will look like. Another church teaches tithing, but takes that teaching to the next level, saying that since tithing is a financial practice, it will result in financial blessings. The Bible teaches that what we sow we reap. If we are sowing finances, we will reap finances. The question is one of emphasis. Evangelical churches teach tithing; charismatic churches teach tithing. One teaches that when we tithe God will bless us in some unnamed way. The other teaches that when we tithe the Lord will bless us financially. It is not really very different from the different stances churches take on the second coming or eternal security or other issues of Bible doctrine.

The cultural difference is in how churches approach their worship of God. Some evangelical churches see God as someone to be feared. The road to righteousness is narrow and we must always be weary of falling short of the mark and meeting a vengeful God. Their music often tells of how things will be better when we finally escape this world of woe.

Charismatic churches have a tradition of teaching that we are children of a loving Father God who desires that we be blessed in our lives here on earth. At Lakewood one of the most popular songs is "I Am a Friend of God." This song celebrates our positive relationship with God. Those who criticize Joel are just people who take a different approach to this teaching and don't approve of those who are not like them.

PROSPERITY GOSPEL

The approach of Joel and Lakewood to prosperity is very balanced; even some of his critics agree on this. Joel does not tell people to simply sit and wait for God to bless them. He does not teach them to go around expecting that God is going to give them a four-thousand-square-foot home or a Mercedes Benz. Joel teaches his people to be faithful to God in every area of their lives: church, family, and job. This teaching is reinforced by the myriad of classes provided to the church membership. In recent bulletins at Lakewood, free classes have been offered in creating individual financial plans and achieving your dreams by overcoming your fears and hardships. Each year, before April 15, free tax preparation assistance is provided. There are classes entitled "How to Become the Lender and Not the Borrower." The purpose of these classes is to help people determine how they can get out of debt. There are classes for men to learn how to be better fathers by being the spiritual priest of their home and a better provider for their family. There are classes for women on how to make the best of the resources God has given them.

In short, Lakewood teaches people to expect the best, as well as to plan and work for the best. It is this balanced approach that changes lives. Joel does not stand in the pulpit and guilt people into giving so they can be blessed. He does not tell people to give financially to Lakewood or they will not have the funds to pay their bills. He teaches that God honors the faithfulness of His people.

Lakewood teaches the same thing that thousands of evangelical churches across America teach from their pulpits.

> *"Bring all the tithes into the storehouse, that there may be food in My house, and try Me now in this," says the* LORD *of hosts, "if I will not open for you the windows of heaven and pour out for you such blessing that there will not be room enough to receive it."* (Malachi 3:10)

Lakewood not only teaches its people to tithe, but it also instructs people in how to make the best use of the 90 percent that remains. People are taught that if they are faithful and wisely use the resources God has given them, they will find their lives better in the future than they are today. This is not only scripturally sound, but it is also pragmatically sound.

An additional part of the prosperity message is what is often called "Word of Faith." "Name it and claim it," "Speak it and see it," "Gab it and grab it"—these are just some of the phrases used by those who do not appreciate this teaching.

When John was filled with the Spirit, he studied the Bible and accepted this teaching as genuine. When Dodie was healed of cancer, she studied the Bible and would not allow any negative words to come out of her mouth. They taught their children to believe in the power of the words that came out of their mouths. They believed in the passages of Scripture such as these:

The disciples came to Jesus privately and said, "Why could we not cast [the demon] out?" So Jesus said to them, "Because of your unbelief; for assuredly, I say to you, if you have faith as a mustard seed, you will say to this mountain, 'Move from here to there,' and it will move; and nothing will be impossible for you." (Matthew 17:19–20)

The key phrase is *"say to this mountain"*! In the next chapter another principle is taught:

Assuredly, I say to you, whatever you bind on earth will be bound in heaven, and whatever you loose on earth will be loosed in heaven. Again I say to you that if two of you agree on earth concerning anything that they ask, it will be done for them by My Father in heaven.
(Matthew 18:18–19)

Another passage that speaks very definitely about the Word of God is:

> *For the word of God is living and powerful, and sharper than any two-edged sword, piercing even to the division of soul and spirit, and of joints and marrow, and is a discerner of the thoughts and intents of the heart.* (Hebrews 4:12)

The Word of Faith doctrine is closely related to the prosperity doctrine. It teaches that we have a God who not only wants to bless us, but He wants to empower us as well. This empowerment teaching is the heart and soul of the charismatic movement. Evangelicals often teach that the time of miracles died with the close of the New Testament writings, and that we now live in a time when we have the Word of God and have no need for miracles in our lives.

The Word of Faith movement believes that God wants to empower His people in mighty ways so that miracles will be a natural result of the Christian life. In the New Testament, the apostles spoke to disease and physical ailments and commanded them to leave. They were speaking words in faith. They were obeying the Scripture that taught that what we bind on earth will be bound in heaven and what we loose on earth will be loosed in heaven. The charismatic tradition believes and teaches that these words are active and have power. Other traditions believe that these words are only words and have no power at all.

Joel teaches and believes that what we say has a direct impact on what happens in our lives. The Bible teaches this as well:

> *Brood of vipers! How can you, being evil, speak good things? For out of the abundance of the heart the mouth speaks. A good man out of the good treasure of his heart brings forth good things, and an evil man out of the evil treasure brings*

forth evil things. But I say to you that for every idle word men
may speak, they will give account of it in the day of judgment.
For by your words you will be justified, and by your words
you will be condemned.   (Matthew 12:34–37)

Joel teaches that we can spew forth poison from our
mouths or sweet blessings. The choice is ours. Some may disagree with the teaching, but they are really voicing a difference in the interpretation of the Scripture.

JOEL'S STYLE

Another frequent criticism of Lakewood revolves around
the style of the Sunday morning service. Some people regard
the type of service and style of message as a "seeker service," a
style popularized by Bill Hybels and the Willow Creek Community Church in the Chicago area, and also promoted by
Rick Warren and Saddleback Community Church in Southern California. It focuses on upbeat music and a message that
strives to address the needs in the daily lives of people. It also
strives to present a service where nonbelievers or "spiritual
seekers" would not be intimidated and would feel welcome.
This style of service suggests that the purpose of the weekend
services is to bring nonbelievers into the church so they can be
exposed to the things of the kingdom. Classes and services for
the purpose of developing spiritual maturity and discipling
believers in a strong relationship with Jesus Christ are held at
other times.

In truth, the services at Lakewood do use many of the
same tactics as seeker services. Joel strongly believes that it
is his job to give the people who come to church on the weekend something to build their lives upon. He tells them how
the Bible and the Christian life can be applied to everyday

life. He preaches about how a Christian should live in such a way as to have a better relationship with family, friends, and coworkers. He tells people how God wants to assist them in the challenges of life.

This leads us to a futhre criticism that accuses Lakewood services of being quality entertainment, but little else. Many such critics will admit that they have never attended a Lakewood service and that they prefer a service with a more traditional approach. Yet, in many ways, the Lakewood service is very traditional. It has a song service, followed by a time of prayer for the individual needs of the people, followed by an inspirational piece, often performed by the choir or a small group, and on some occasions a solo. Joel then delivers a sermon about a half hour in length, which concludes with an opportunity for people to receive Jesus Christ as their Savior. Is this really that different from thousands of other services at churches across the country? But Lakewood tends to get more attention than many because of its size, its television exposure, and the incredible quality with which it presents the service.

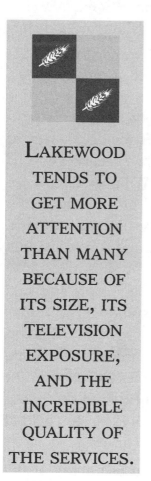

LAKEWOOD TENDS TO GET MORE ATTENTION THAN MANY BECAUSE OF ITS SIZE, ITS TELEVISION EXPOSURE, AND THE INCREDIBLE QUALITY OF THE SERVICES.

The music of Lakewood is not the style found in every church. But again, styles of worship are a matter of cuture. The charismatic or Pentecostal style of worship encourages worshippers to celebrate what the Lord has done in their lives here on earth. Many of the traditional hymns sung by more traditional evangelical churches speak of the life in the hereafter once this "trail of tears" has been endured here on earth. Again, it is a matter of emphasis and tradition. The Lakewood music team is as talented as any secular musicians the world has to offer. This may offend some as seeming showy, but apologizing for presenting the best when we worship the Lord does not seem right either. For those who don't like this tradition, Lakewood's music will just not be appreciated. Again, it seems to be more a matter of style, not substance.

JOEL'S THEOLOGY

The evangelical tradition preaches that we must embrace God in order to avoid eternal damnation. Charismatic churches, such as Lakewood, teach that we must embrace God because of the changes He brings to our lives here on earth. Gaining heaven and avoiding hell is a marvelous side benefit, but it doesn't have much to offer the believer who desires to live an abundant and overcoming life on this earth. In the New Testament, Jesus spoke more often about the marvelous things God brings to the lives of those who love Him than about eternal damnation.

Joel's view of Christianity agrees with basic Christian doctrine. He views the Bible as divinely inspired and without error. He believes that God created the universe, that Jesus Christ was the only Son of God, that He lived and performed miracles on earth, that He died on the cross for our sins, rose from the dead on the third day, ascended into heaven, where He sits at the right hand of God the Father, and will one day literally return to earth and judge the living and the dead. But some want to concentrate upon the few differences instead of the many similarities.

In an interview with *Outreach* magazine, respected Foursquare pastor and denominational leader Jack Hayford discussed this situation. "In North America, I think—and I say this cautiously, I can't say it casually because it is such a grievous thing to me—the commitment of some sectors of the church to divide breaches the freedom of the Spirit. And it exists as a commitment to division—in the name of righteousness. We judge people as unworthy because they don't have the insight we do or they don't follow our model."[133]

JOEL'S MEDIA MISCUES

Whenever Joel is interviewed in the media, his words are endlessly dissected and replayed for possible errors. As mentioned before, Joel's most infamous appearance was the 2005 interview with Larry King on his CNN program. Joel misspoke, and his error was triumphed over by those who do not appreciate Joel's style in the first place, as proof of his lack of doctrinal purity. That Joel made a major mistake cannot be questioned. He quickly issued an apology for his statements. When Larry King asked him if Muslims or Jews were going to heaven, Joel tried to fall back on Matthew 7:1, *"Judge not, that you be not judged."* He was trying to say that whether anyone went to heaven or not was not Joel Osteen's decision; it was the decision of God alone. In doing so, he seemed to imply that there was a chance for any religious people to get to heaven. His words were instantly proclaimed across the Internet and in the Christian press, forcing Joel to issue the retraction.

As I wrote earlier, during the King interview, Larry asked Joel a series of questions designed to create headlines. He asked Joel about the prosperity gospel. Joel responded there was more to prosperity than money—that God wants to bless His people with health and successful careers as well. King asked him questions about abortion and same-sex marriage, hot-button political issues. Joel fought them off, answering that he thought abortions and same-sex marriages were not the best way for people to live their lives, but it was not his job to condemn people. Joel said that Lakewood was available for anyone who wanted to worship God, regardless of the problems they had faced in their lives.

In truth, just as many people tune into NASCAR races to view a crash, there are a number of people around the country who watch people like Joel for the purpose of seeing them make a mistake. Joel understands that he must be true to the calling God has placed on his life. It is his task to bring the love of God for His people to as many people as he can.

JOEL'S LIFESTYLE

Another frequent target of criticism concerns the Osteen's personal life, especially their lifestyle. Much has been made of the home where Joel, Victoria, and their children live. Joel and Victoria have been married for nearly twenty years. When they were younger and first married, they lived in a condominium, but as they grew older they purchased their first house. They purchased a house that needed work on a large lot in a very good Houston neighborhood. They spent all of their extra money and time in remodeling their home, doing as much of the work themselves as they could. Once the house was remodeled they received an offer to split the lot into two parcels. Joel and Victoria were able to keep the second lot. They made a good return on their original investment, and with the money they earned, they built the house where they live now. All of this was done before Joel became pastor of the church.

Today, this home has a value in excess of two million dollars. Some struggle with the idea of a pastor living in a home with a value this high. But they are questioning a home that Joel and Victoria had before they went into the pastorate and that they built with funds they earned outside the ministry. The only way they could have avoided this criticism would have been to sell the house after Joel became senior pastor and move into a less expensive home. This would seem to be an extreme reaction for someone living in a house they lived in before entering the ministry. It also seems extreme considering Joel stopped taking compensation from the church after his book became a best seller.

CHURCH IN A SPORTING ARENA

Another controversial aspect of Lakewood actually involves the building. Since the church moved into the former Compaq Center in July 2005, there have been a number of comments regarding the lack of a cross either in the sanctuary or on the building. But this same criticism has been made about a number of megachurch buildings across America. There is no cross on Saddleback Church in California, nor is there one on Willow Creek Community Church near Chicago. These churches have built campuses that look more like college campuses than churches, turning off many traditionalists.

At Lakewood, a big globe of the world sits behind Joel as he preaches—similar to the globe used at the old location in East Houston. It is a symbol of the world that Jesus Christ died for. It is a symbol of the world that Lakewood Church spends millions of dollars trying to touch every week. There is no cross on the outside of the building because the Compaq Center was a sporting arena before Lakewood moved into it. It was not a cathedral then, and it isn't one now. It is simply a place for people to come and find God.

One of the problems with churches today is that they intimidate people who are in need of God. This is something that many Christians don't understand or appreciate. People think they have to meet a certain standard before they can approach God. Joel Osteen and Lakewood understand that we do not have to meet any standard before we meet God. God embraces us and brings us up to His standard. We come to Him just as we are. He does the changing within us. We don't have to change ourselves. If churches today would communicate this message to the world, perhaps our vacant churches would begin to fill with people once again.

GOES WITH THE TERRITORY

Many of the issues Joel and Lakewood face today have been around for a long time. John preached on the blessings of God before he passed away. The church was well known in the Houston area; it was a large church and had a large television ministry before Joel became pastor. Yet, since Joel took over leadership, these issues have attracted attention around the country because Lakewood is now the largest church in America, having services in the largest church sanctuary in America, with the largest television ministry of any local church in the world.

It is the old adage: if you want to draw attention to yourself, stick your head above the crowd. By simply being faithful to the things that God has called them to do, Lakewood

The Rise of Lakewood Church and Joel Osteen

Church and Joel Osteen as pastor have drawn the attention of the nation and particularly the Christian world, and the criticism that comes with it. Then again, even Jesus was criticized by the religious leaders of His time, as well as His own family, so maybe this just goes along with the territory.

chapter twenty-three

FROM OBSCURITY TO PROMINENCE

Examine me, O LORD, and prove me; try my mind and my heart. For Your lovingkindness is before my eyes, and I have walked in Your truth.
—Psalm 26:2–3

J oel Osteen rose from virtual anonymity to a man of major influence in both the Christian and secular worlds in less than seventy-two months. His meteoric rise is unlike any other in recent history. The closest comparison in the last sixty years is Dr. Billy Graham, who went from holding Youth for Christ revivals after World War II to visiting President Truman in the White House within about the same period of time. Some would say that to compare Joel Osteen to Billy Graham is absurd, but those around him don't think so, the media doesn't think so, and others around the country are beginning to think about the comparison.[134] Is Joel Osteen the Billy Graham of his generation? Billy Graham is not a position to be filled, but for nearly two hundred years the Lord has raised up a man in each generation to be a leader and impact that generation. There is a straight line from Charles Finney to D. L. Moody to Billy Sunday to Billy Graham. Who will be that man for this generation?

Joel's sister, Lisa, has her own opinion: "The reason they [compare Joel to Graham] is that they have the anointing to bring thousands, and that's what we saw with Billy Graham, and still see today. This is only the hand of God on a person. You don't choose that. God chooses."[135]

Why do people respond to Joel? Paul Osteen says he is asked that all the time, and although his younger brother is too modest to admit it, the reason is Joel Osteen himself. Joel is the reason why the church has gotten so popular. Joel is the reason why Lakewood has the top-rated Christian show in broadcasting. Joel is the reason why they've gotten so big that they've added services and needed to make the Compaq Center move.[136] John Osteen birthed the church, but it is Joel Osteen who can't seem to stop bringing them in.

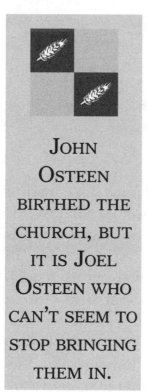

JOHN OSTEEN BIRTHED THE CHURCH, BUT IT IS JOEL OSTEEN WHO CAN'T SEEM TO STOP BRINGING THEM IN.

Cindy Cruse-Ratliff was asked what it was like to work with Joel. "What a great man, he is humble, but very bold, quiet, but not timid. The definition of meek is, 'power under control,' that's Pastor Joel."[137]

The national media is recognizing the gifts of Joel Osteen in ways that few men, religious or otherwise, have been described. The *Washington Post* calls him the hottest commodity in multimedia today. They likened him to Billy Graham in terms of appeal if not message. They also asked Joel about his message and why he presents it so: "For a long time, churches beat people down. People are in need of inspiration and encouragement. So many negative voices are pulling us down during the week. People really want you to tell them there is a great future in front of you, you can leave your past behind."[138] It could have been the articles in the *Washington Post* or perhaps just happenstance, but when Joel met White House presidential advisor Karl Rove, he went to introduce himself and Rove said, "You don't have to introduce yourself to me. I watch you every Sunday on TV."[139]

Business Week describes Joel as one of a new generation of evangelical entrepreneurs transforming their branch of Protestantism into one of the fastest-growing and most influential religious groups in America.[140] In 2004, *The Church Report*, a Christian monthly magazine, named the fifty most influential Christians in America. Joel was listed at number five behind President Bush, Mel Gibson, Billy Graham, and Rick Warren, and just in front of T. D. Jakes.[141] The year before, *Church Executive* magazine listed its fifty most influential Christians in America, and he wasn't even on the list. That same year, *Ministries Today* listed Joel among the top twenty influencers in the Pentecostal and charismatic community. By 2006, Joel was named as the second most influential Christian in America behind only T. D. Jakes and ahead of Billy Graham and the president, among others.[142] What an amazing ascension in power and influence in the Christian world. Joel went from being unlisted to second on the list in less than four years.

Other major media outlets use similar phrases to describe the ministry of Joel Osteen. There are detractors, of course, but the rise of Joel Osteen and Lakewood Church in such a relatively short period of time is nothing short of miraculous. There is no other way to describe it.

The Rise of Lakewood Church and Joel Osteen

But Joel Osteen is far more than a media creation. There is a great deal of substance behind the man. He takes the responsibility of reaching the city of Houston through Lakewood Church and touching the world through the television ministry and arena services very seriously. Joel understands the task before him. One article noted that the great popular preachers of history, like Charles Finney, D. L. Moody, Billy Sunday, and Billy Graham, have shared three characteristics: a good organization, a distinctive and appealing personality, and an easily grasped message. Added to this could be unquestioned integrity. These four men ministered to their generations without serious scandal or serious public embarrassment. After the televangelist scandals of the 1980s with Jim Bakker and Jimmy Swaggert, this issue has taken on even more importance.

JOEL'S ORGANIZATION

The organization that Joel has assembled in just a few short years has quickly risen to meet a very high standard. A ministry does not grow to become the largest church in America, and at the same time build the largest television ministry in the world, and at the same time refurbish and take possession of the largest church auditorium in the United States, without having a team that cannot be matched. Once more, Joel is the man who put this team together.

Joel has assigned his team the tasks that accomplish the mission and goals of the church. Everyone has a role to play, respects one another, and takes his or her own task seriously. This team has built an organization unparalleled in any church in America. Documents show revenue for the 2004 fiscal year of fifty-four million dollars including three million four hundred thousand dollars from the church bookstore.[143] Church administrator Kevin Comes said, "We have an incredible budget system. We budget all the way down to hot chocolate." Joel understands the seriousness of this responsibility. He was quoted as saying, "It would be naïve to say, 'No we are not in business.' We obviously are a business because we are dealing with millions of dollars. And I say that because we do not take that lightly."

Time will tell if the organization that Joel has put together will work as a team for a short time or for decades. They are, for the most part, young adults in their thirties and forties. One of the marks of a great organization is longevity. One can hardly think of Billy Graham without also thinking of Cliff Barrows or George Beverly Shea. They and many others in the Billy Graham organization have been together for over fifty years. If they stick it out, Joel Osteen's team could easily be together for thirty years or more.

JOEL'S PERSONALITY

The second characteristic is a distinctive and appealing personality. Joel comes across as a sincere and caring young man, whether in person or on television. He has been described as a spiritual leader, motivational speaker, and celebrity. There can be no question that Joel is a distinctive personality as the senior pastor of a megachurch and as pastor to the world. Through television, Joel comes across as energetic and youthful looking. The stories about his wife and children, as well as about his brother, mother, and sisters, appeal to people of all ages, and all economic and ethnic backgrounds. Because of his willingness to tell on himself, he does not come across as a perfect man, but as a man striving to be the best that he can be. His way of starting his sermons with a joke, often sent to him over the Internet from a member or viewer, allows everyone to see his sense of humor. The fact that not all these jokes are religious or take religion seriously makes him all the more appealing and accessible. That he gets emotional when speaking about his dad or about caring for someone who came to him with a need makes him seem like a real person, not someone who puts on a persona for the television camera. It is amazing that a man who has built the kind of organization that he has, and has come so far in so little time, can still seem humble. But he does.

A recent article described Joel as a man who, no matter how busy, seems to have all the time in the world for you. He comes across as a small town pastor. His manners and politeness seem to come from genuine cheerfulness rather than celebrity charm. He seems as if he wants to connect.[144]

This personality of compassion and genuine concern is communicated to people whether in person at a book signing, in a media interview, or on television in a sermon to millions. He has become one of the most influential and powerful pastors in America, but he seems to have accepted the mantle with humility and grace.

JOEL'S MESSAGE

Joel preaches a message of hope to all, and he does so unapologetically. But the proof that his message resonates with his audience is in the response he receives. It would be easy to say that eighteen thousand people walked the aisle to receive Christ as their Savior in 2004 at the East Houston location. A *New York Times* article quoted several people who enjoyed Joel's messages, people from all walks of life who attested to how the message had changed their lives. One man, who described himself as a "hard core" Catholic, said, "He's added a different dimension to our spiritual life. We're always quoting Joel's talks in our daily lives." Another man said that the church had taught him to name the things he wanted, and that he would receive them. "The Bible says, speak those things that aren't as if they are." "Now I'm speaking my marriage to Isabelle," he said, gesturing to his girlfriend. "And having a relationship with my children. The Bible tells me that as long as I serve Him, I shall have what I want. The reason I didn't name material things is that I know I'm here on borrowed time from God."[145]

Joel's message seems to reach people all across the nation. One woman in Braintree, Massachusetts, said, "My family watches Joel every Sunday morning before we go to ten o'clock mass. He's uplifting and positive. It's not like you're doomed to death. He makes you realize that no matter what you've done, God forgives you. I need that in my life right now."

In Philadelphia, a woman in line to get her book autographed said, "Most preachers you hear make you feel bad about yourself and they talk about the worst part of yourself. Joel Osteen talks about the best part of yourself."[146] Statements like this show that Joel is becoming a huge force in Christianity as he reaches out to people far beyond the standard Christian market.

JOEL IS BECOMING A HUGE FORCE IN CHRISTIANITY AS HE REACHES OUT TO PEOPLE FAR BEYOND THE STANDARD CHRISTIAN MARKET.

JOEL'S INTEGRITY

The final characteristic that sets Joel apart from so many and makes his ministry unique is integrity. It simply is not possible for a man like Joel Osteen to fly under the radar. There are many who would like to find a scandal in someone so public. Olie Anthony, who has made a career of exposing corruption in ministries, admitted that he does not agree theologically with everything that Joel says, but he still cannot find fault with his honesty and integrity. "There is no hint of fraud or wrongdoing or false promises, per se, or inducements to give money. There is none of that in him and I applaud him for that." Anthony went on to say, "We have never had any, any even hint of fraud in his activities and he's doing it extremely well obviously."[147]

When Joel went to The Palace in Auburn Hill, Michigan, WXYZ-TV 7 in Detroit did an investigation into Joel and his ministry. The investigative reporter, Steve Wilson, cited Joel's lack of a seminary degree and apparent lack of training to lead Lakewood. But he also admitted that the church had grown exponentially since Joel had assumed leadership. He noted that Lakewood was planning to spend ninety million dollars to refurbish the former Compaq Center. He said that Lakewood had better television equipment than any station for which he had worked. But he also admitted there was no hint that Joel himself was misusing any of the seventy-five million or more that was expected to flow through the ministry. Wilson noted these additional facts: Even though it was not required, Joel released two years of audited financial statements to the press and other interested parties. His home is not an average middle-class home, but Joel and Victoria purchased it before he became pastor with their own money. In addition, although he could legally declare the home a parsonage and take it off the tax rolls, he voluntarily paid the $25,329 tax bill with his own money. Joel admits to traveling first class and staying in nice hotel suites, but the investigation showed that everything was paid for with Joel's personal credit card. Wilson finally noted that the worst thing anyone has accused Joel of is being more of a motivational speaker than a true preacher of the gospel. But the investigative reporter had to admit, "My own mother and millions of others love this guy." [148]

The question then becomes, what assurance is there that in the future Joel will maintain this level of integrity? The answer lies in his background. Joel grew up in a pastor's home where there was unquestioned integrity. He noted this on Vision Sunday when he became the senior pastor. Joel perceives Lakewood and the television ministry to be a sacred trust given to him. Dodie reinforced this idea when she told what she had always said to her children: "Daddy's name was always squeaky clean, and we intend to keep it that way. They are so respectful of their father and of me. You don't hear much criticism about Lakewood Church or about the Osteen family."[149]

The last portion of her statement also brings out an aspect of Joe's support system that ensures his integrity as well as anything could. One of the problems with people of power is that they get to the place where no one can question them regarding anything about their decisions or motives for what they do. As the old story goes, nobody will tell the emperor that he has no clothes. This does not seem to be the case with Joel. When someone comes to a position of authority, having been born into a family with such a legacy as that of John Osteen, he sees his position as a God-given trust that must not be violated. Joel Osteen has not surrounded himself with "yes men." He is surrounded by close family members who have no problem telling truth to power. When no one on earth can talk straight to you, your family always can.

Joel and his siblings, Paul and Lisa, have accepted their roles at Lakewood as continuing in the sacred trust that was created by their father. Joel makes references to his father in many of his sermons and his memory is never far away. From the videos that tell of the beginning of the church to the many books and tapes by John Osteen available in the bookstore, no one is pushing his memory aside. Dodie attends every service, and many of the services across the country. There is never a question that she is not involved in the ongoing activities of Joel and the church. The involvement of Paul and Lisa is not hidden either. The video screens are constantly announcing events at which they will be speaking.

The Osteen family does not see this arrangement as a problem but as a positive thing. Lisa spoke about the family and their responsibilities at Lakewood. "Yes, the family is in charge. The board is all family members. Joel decides what he feels like the Lord wants him to do, but we work with attorneys. We call other ministries. We get as much counsel as we can. We have a great accountability to the Lord and to the people and we feel that. We hold ourselves to a high standard."[150]

Paul also spoke about the family's responsibilities as the leaders of Lakewood. "The beauty of our organization is that we don't have to pass things by a thousand boards or a bunch of people with different opinions. If we want to add an extra service next week, we can do it. There's a real beauty about the way we work together. We know our parts. It sounds a lot like the body of Christ."[151]

Some will be apprehensive about the Osteen family's role in the operation of Lakewood Church. But there is one thing to consider when studying the situation. Operating a church with a budget of over fifty-five million dollars and growing, and being responsible for the day-to-day ministry needs of over thirty thousand people and growing, is a task that no one in this country has ever encountered before. Many have an opinion about how it should be done, but no one can speak from experience. Lakewood is blazing a trail where no one has ever walked before. Until one has walked this path, it is difficult to speak or offer opinions authoritatively.

LAKEWOOD IS BLAZING A TRAIL WHERE NO ONE HAS EVER WALKED BEFORE.

Joel Osteen is accountable to the membership of Lakewood Church. They show their approval by their faithfulness in attendance and offerings. People always have the option to walk away with their pocketbooks if they disapprove of what is taking place. Joel Osteen is responsible to his family, who see their role as stewards of the trust created by their father. Will this trust be handed down to the next generation of the Osteen family? Only God knows, and time will tell.

Joel operates as the chief executive officer of Lakewood Church as a corporation. He has responsibility for all major decisions and the overall vision of the church. As such, he directs the activities of Duncan Dodd and Don Iloff and the other two hundred staff members of Lakewood Church. Joel performs no weddings or funerals, makes no hospital visits, does no pastoral counseling, and turns down outside speaking engagements. His primary task is preaching. This is what ministers to the thousands who attend the weekly services and to the seven million or more who watch by television all over the world. Joel spends all day Wednesday and Thursday preparing that week's sermon. Then he spends two half-days practicing and polishing the sermon until he has it down cold.

"It takes a lot more work than just getting up there with an outline and preaching to people who know your heart, but this is a responsibility, so I'm very careful. It takes the majority of my time. It's basically what I do."[152] By the time he is finished with the sermon, it is written out nearly word for word and will be about twenty-six minutes long. That is the perfect length of time for a half-hour television show with an opening, closing, and invitation. Joel spends three days preparing his sermon and a Saturday night and Sunday morning delivering the sermon four times.

In the corporate world, there are certain businesses that have stood as family businesses for generations. Johnson and Johnson and Ford Motor Company come to mind. Both have been around for a century or more. Today a family member heads each of these companies. For Johnson and Johnson, it is the fifth generation and, for Ford, it is the fourth generation. The individuals who have the responsibility to direct the activities of the company regard this to be a trust placed in them by the family. In Christianity, there are no modern equivalents. There are fathers and sons who are each pastors of megachurches. But the idea of a son succeeding his father, surrounded by his siblings, is unique to evangelical Christianity today. But who is to say this was not the plan of God when He called John Osteen into the full-gospel movement before Joel was born? God has used families before. After all, who was Isaac but the son of Abraham? Jacob, but the son of Isaac? Joseph, but the son of Jacob? And yet, for nearly thirty centuries people have spoken of the God of Abraham, Isaac, and Jacob.

Again, Joel Osteen understands that it is his task to maintain the sacred trust that has been placed in his hands. This may be the ultimate accountability that helps Joel Osteen remain a man of integrity. He may make mistakes in his life, but he will always strive to do his best to care for the trust that he has been given.

Lakewood Church has come a long way. Who would have believed that the little feed store church led by a former Baptist preacher would one day develop into one of the leading Christian influences around the world—and a ministry that still bears the family name? If Hollywood had written the story, no one would have believed it could be true. But then, God has a tendency to write history with the most unlikely of people and circumstances.

The world continues to watch Lakewood Church with fascination. The media can question Joel about his goals and the success of his ministry. Others may have a distaste for Joel's methods. Critics will analyze the Osteens' every move. Meanwhile, God will continue to write the story of Joel Osteen and Lakewood Church, day by day, one changed life at a time.

ENDNOTES

Chapter 1: God Calls Out His Servant

[1] Sam Martin, *How I Led One and One Led a Million* (Houston: Sam Martin, 2001), 3–4.

[2] John Osteen, *Rivers of Living Waters* (Houston: John Osteen Publishing, 1975), 7.

[3] John Osteen, *Keep What God Gives* (Houston: John Osteen Publishing, 1980), 20.

[4] John Osteen, *Believing God for Your Loved Ones* (Houston: John Osteen Publishing, 1988), 16–17.

[5] Joel Osteen, *Daily Readings from Your Best Life Now: 90 Devotions for Living at Your Full Potential* (New York: Warner Faith, 2005), 182.

[6] Ibid., 25.

[7] John Osteen, *A Miracle for Your Marriage* (Houston: John Osteen Publishing, 1988), 25.

[8] John Osteen, *Love & Marriage* (Houston: John Osteen Publishing, 1980), 17.

[9] Dodie Osteen, *Choosing Life One Day at a Time* (Houston: Dodie Osteen Publishing, 2001).

Chapter 2: The Spirit Begins to Move

[10] Ibid., 27.

[11] John Osteen, *How to Flow in the Super Supernatural* (Houston: John Osteen Publishing, 1972), 25.

[12] John Osteen, *This Awakening Generation* (Houston: John Osteen Publishing, 1973), 25.

[13] John Osteen, *Rivers of Living Waters* (Houston: John Osteen Publishing, 1975), 21.

Chapter 3: God Is Awesome, But Not Everyone Believes

[14] Ibid., 55.

[15] John Osteen, *The Truth Shall Set You Free* (Houston: John Osteen Publishing, 1978), 18–19.

[16] John Osteen, *How to Minister Healing to the Sick* (Houston: John Osteen Publishing, 1981), 25.

[17] Bill Shepson, "He's Doing His Father's Business," *Charisma*, August 2000, 77.

Chapter 4: Houston and the World

[18] Tim Dillard, *The Lakewood Story* (Bellaire, Texas: Dillard Local Branding, 2002), http://www.dillardlocalbranding.com /gcg/ lakewood.html (June, 2006).

[19] John Osteen, *How to Flow in the Super Supernatural* (Houston: John Osteen Publishing, 1972), 44.

Chapter 5: Mary's Miracle

[20] John Osteen, *The Divine Flow* (Houston: John Osteen Publishing, 1978), 24–25.

[21] John Osteen, *You Can Change Your Destiny* (Houston: John Osteen Publishing, 1968), 52.

[22] John Osteen, *The Divine Flow*, 25.

[23] John Osteen, *You Can Change Your Destiny*, 54.

[24] John Osteen, *Pulling Down Strongholds* (Houston: John Osteen Publishing, 1988), 16.

[25] John Osteen, *You Can Change Your Destiny*, 54–55.

[26] John Osteen, *The Divine Flow*, 26–27.

Chapter 6: God Blesses Lakewood

[27] Lisa Osteen, *Overcoming Oppositon: How to Succeed in Doing the Will of God* (Houston: John Osteen Publishing, 1990), 12.

[28] Joel Osteen, *Your Best Life Now: 7 Steps to Living at Your Full Potential* (New York: Warner Faith, 2004), 23.

[29] L. Osteen, *Overcoming Oppositon:*, 12.

[30] Julia Duin, "Lakewood's New Building to Get Classy Send-off," *Houston Chronicle*, April 9, 1988.

Chapter 7: Dodie's Battle

[31] John Osteen, sermon audio tape, "Secrets of Building a Great Local Church," Lakewood Church, 1994.

[32] John Osteen, *Unraveling the Mystery of the Blood Covenant* (Houston: John Osteen Publishing, 1987), 58.

[33] Author's note: Dodie's testimony is found in so many places that it is impossible to give proper credit to all of them, but I would like to make reference to the following:

Dodie Osteen, *Choosing Life One Day at a Time* (Houston: Lakewood Church, 2001).

Joel Osteen, *Your Best Life Now: 7 Steps to Living at Your Full Potential* (New York: Warner Faith, 2004), 126–127, 162.

Joel Osteen, *Your Best Life Now Journal: A Guide to Reaching Your Full Potential* (New York: Warner Faith, 2005), 79.

Joel Osteen, *Your Best Life Now: 90 Daily Readings for Living at Your Full Potential* (New York: Warner Faith, 2005), 148–150.

Dodie Osteen, *Healed of Cancer* (Houston: John Osteen Publishing, 1983), 5–29.

John Osteen, *Seven Qualities of a Man of Faith* (Houston: John Osteen Publishing, 1990), 28.

John Osteen, *Unraveling the Mystery of the Blood Covenant* (Houston: John Osteen Publishing, 1987), 58.

Dodie Osteen, sermon audio tape, "Healed of Cancer," Lakewood Church.

Chapter 8: Lakewood Takes to the Air

[34] Jennifer Mathieu, "Power House," *Houston Press*, April 4, 2002.

[35] Julia Duin, "Oasis of Love: Lakewood Congregation Plans Houston's Largest Sanctuary," *Houston Chronicle*, February 14, 1987.

[36] Mike McDaniel, "The Tube Sticks Around/Channel 55 Owner Joel Osteen Has No Plans to Sell Station," *Houston Chronicle*, October 6, 1999.

[37] Mike McDaniel, "Channel 55 Launches with Vintage Shows, Fresh Attitude," *Houston Chronicle*, October 12, 1999.

[38] McDaniel, "The Tube Sticks Around/Channel 55 Owner Joel Osteen Has No Plans To Sell Station."

Chapter 9: The Lakewood Legacy

[39] Joel Osteen, *Living the Joy Filled Life* (Houston: Joel Osteen Ministries, 2005), 7–8.

[40] R. A. Dyer, Rad Sallee, & Eric Hanson, "Church Bomb Probers Question Ex-Husband," *Houston Chronicle*, February 8, 1990.

[41] Elmer L. Towns, John N. Vaughan, and David J. Seifert, *The Complete Book of Church Growth* (Wheaton, Illinois: Tyndale House Publishers, Inc., 1987 Edition), 351.

[42] Ibid. 360.

[43] Edythe Draper, ed., *The Almanac of the Christian World* (Wheaton, Illinois: Tyndale House Publishers, 1993–1994 Edition), 361.

[44] Dodie Osteen, *Choosing Life One Day at a Time* (Houston: Lakewood Church, 2001), 57.

[45] Ibid., 59.

Chapter 10: The End of an Era

[46] Armnando Villafranca and Cecile S. Holmes, "Worshippers Fondly Remember Lakewood Church Pastor's Integrity, Stand for Christ," *Houston Chronicle*, January 25, 1999.

[47] William Martin, "Prime Minister," *Texas Monthly*, August 2005.

Chapter 11: A Vision for the Future

[48] Cecile S. Holmes, "Stepping into the Pulpit, Joel Osteen Prepared to Fill Big Shoes," *Houston Chronicle*, October 3, 1999.

Chapter 12: Joel's Leadership Builds a Team

[49] John C. Maxwell, *The 17 Indisputable Laws of Teamwork* (Nashville: Thomas Nelson Publishers, 2001), 1.

[50] Ibid., 110.

[51] http://www.integritymusic.com/new/artist/0502.html (June, 2006).

[52] http://www.gospelflava.com/articles/cindycruseratcliff.html (May, 2006).

[53] Kristi Watts and Julie Blim, "Israel Houghton: An Intimate Portrait of Worship," *The 700 Club*, December 5, 2004.

[54] Ibid.

[55] Nola Warren, *The Foolishness of God* (Lake Mary, Florida: Creation House Press, 2000), 54–55.

[56] Tara Dooley, "Iglesia Lakewood," *Houston Chronicle*, July 16, 2005.

[57] Ibid.

Chapter 13: Joel's Vision for Sundays

[58] http://news.crossman.com/story/praise-be-the-music/689.html (June, 2006).

[59] Helen Tse, "Nine Systems Publishing Solutions Power Joel Osteen into The Top 100 Most Popular Podcasts at iTunes," May 31, 2006, http://www.ninesystems.com/company/press/pr5312006.php (June, 2006).

Chapter 14: Joel and Victoria

[60] Joel Osteen, interview with Larry King, *Larry King Live*, CNN, June 20, 2005.

[61] Joel Osteen, "An Evening with Joel Osteen at Madison Square Garden," October 2004.

[62] John C. Roper, "At Lakewood, Goal Is to Be 'Good Stewards' of God's Money," *Houston Chronicle,* July 23, 2005.

[63] Wes Eichenwald, "Opposites Attract: Joel and Victoria Osteen on How They Live Happily Ever After," *Texas Family,* May/June, 32.

[64] Ibid.

[65] William Martin, "Prime Minister," *Texas Monthly,* August 2005.

[66] Eichenwald, "Opposites Attract."

[67] http://shobali.blogspot.com (April, 2006).

[68] Ann Marie Kilday, "Victoria Osteen and the FBI Have Different Views on What Occurred Aboard Airliner," *Houston Chronicle,* December 22, 2005.

[69] Ibid.

Chapter 15: The Osteen Family

[70] http://www.chron.com/CDA/archives/archive.mpl?id=1987_442322 (April, 2006).

[71] Richard Vara, "Throwing Out the First Ball," *Houston Chronicle,* March 13, 1999.

[72] Lisa Comes, sermon, Lakewood Church, May 14, 2006.

[73] Tim Dillard, *The Lakewood Story,* http://www.dillardlocalbranding.com /gcg/lakewood.html (April, 2006).

Chapter 16: Writing a Best Seller

[74] Rachel Donadio, "ESSAY; Faith-Based Publishing," *The New York Times,* November 28, 2004.

[75] Jeremy Desel, "Osteen's Upbeat Message in High Demand," KHOU-TV news, December 13, 2004.

[76] Mary A. Jacobs, "Osteen Shares Steps to Realizing Potential," *The Dallas Morning News,* October 15, 2004.

[77] Joel Osteen, interview by Diana Keough, December 10, 2004. http:// www.bookreporter.com/authors/au-osteen-joel.asp (May 2006).

[78] Ibid.

[79] John A. Zukowski, "The Joel Osteen Phenomenon," *The Newark (NJ) Express-Times,* July 8, 2005.

[80] Douglas LeBlanc, "Thou Shalt Not Be Negative," *Christianity Today,* April 14, 2005.

[81] Karen Holt, "Osteen Keeping the Faith, Agrees to Two More for Warner," *The Book Standard News,* January 27, 2005.

[82] Edward Wyatt, "Religious Broadcaster Gets Rich Contract for Next Book," *The New York Times,* March 15, 2006.

[83] Zukowski, "The Joel Osteen Phenomenon."

[84] Desel, "Osteen's Upbeat Message in High Demand."

[85] Wyatt, " Religious Broadcaster Gets Rich Contract for Next Book."

Chapter 17: Talking to the Press

[86] Byron Pitts, "Selling God a Lucrative Business," *CBS Evening News*, June 28, 2005.

[87] Harry Smith, "Osteen: God Is on Your Side," *The Early Show*, October 21, 2005.

[88] Jamie Gangel, "Charismatic TV Evangelist Aims to Send a Message of Hope and Victory to Followers around the World," *The Today Show*, February 2, 2005.

[89] Tyler Mathisen, "CNBC Examines the Growing Business of Evangelical Christianity," CNBC, April 1, 2005.

[90] "Televangelist Joel Osteen Speaks to 'GMA,'" *ABC News*, October 2005.

[91] "Joel Osteen: The Man behind the Ministry," *Nightline*, ABC, June 16, 2006.

[92] http://transcripts.cnn.com/TRANSCRIPTS/0507/03/lkl.01.html (May 2006).

[93] William C. Symonds, "Online Extra: Meet the Prosperity Preacher," *Business Week*, May 23, 2005, http://www.businessweek.com/magazine/content/05_21/b3934014_mz001.htm (May 2006).

[94] Kris Axtman, "The Rise of the American Megachurch," *The Christian Science Monitor*, December 30, 2003.

[95] Lois Romano, "'The Smiling Preacher' Builds on Large Following," *The Washington Post*, January 30, 2005.

Chapter 18: An Evening with Joel Osteen

[96] Tara Dooley, "Lakewood Trips Target TV Viewers," *Houston Chronicle*, July 3, 2004.

[97] Brett Hoffman, "Tickets Sell Out for Star Evangelist's Dallas Event," *Fort Worth Star-Telegram*, February 24, 2005.

[98] Tara Dooley, "Lakewood Audience Overflows," *Houston Chronicle*, July 17, 2004.

[99] Cathleen Falsani, "What's a Sermon Worth? About $190, Scalpers Say," *The Chicago Sun-Times*, March 4, 2005.

[100] Tara Dooley, "Lakewood Pastor Meets His TV Audience in New York City," *Houston Chronicle*, October 23, 2004.

[101] Jeremy Desel, "Up Close: Houston's Rock Star of a Preacher," KHOU-News 11, December 14, 2004.

[102] Hoffman, "Tickets Sell Out."

[103] Falsani, "What's a Sermon Worth?"

[104] Mary Knox, "What Can We Learn from Ticket Scalpers?" *The Baptist Standard*, April 15, 2005.

[105] Public relations from Feed the Children, "Joel Osteen Teams with Feed the Children to Help Hungry Families across the Country," June 13, 2005.

Chapter 19: The Compaq Center

[106] http://archive.sportingnews.com/nba/articles/20030904/490718.html (April 2006).

[107] http://www.jimgarlow.com/skyline/about_skyline.cfm?pagenum=7 (June 2006).

[108] Eric Berger, "Votes Will Decide Future of More Than One Arena/ Compaq Center Lease Could Go to Area Church," *Houston Chronicle*, October, 29, 2000.

[109] Rosanna Ruiz, "Compaq Center Lease Bid Up for Vote/Lakewood Church's Offer in Millions," *Houston Chronicle*, July 26, 2001.

[110] Mary Flood, "City Council Delays Vote on Compaq Lease," *Houston Chronicle*, July 28, 2001.

[111] Rachel Graves and Mary Flood, "Talks OK'd on Compaq Center Deal/ City to Negotiate with Church," *Houston Chronicle*, July 4, 2001.

[112] Rosanna Ruiz, "Compaq Center Suit Dismissed/Realty Firm Vows Appeal to Stop City from Leasing Site to Church," *Houston Chronicle*, November 22, 2001.

[113] Matt Schwartz, "Compaq Center Lease Deal Near/ Lakewood Church Looks to Have Enough Votes Despite Controversy," *Houston Chronicle*, December 19, 2001.

[114] Matt Schwartz, "Lakewood Deal OK'd By the Council/Church to Rent for $35 Million Over 60 Years," *Houston Chronicle*, December 20, 2001.

[115] Ibid.

[116] Ibid.

[117] JoAnn Zuniga, "Lakewood Deal Faces New Suit/Rival Bidder for Compaq Center Lease Heads to State Court," *Houston Chronicle*, June 12, 2002.

[118] Kristen Mack, "3-Way Deal Clears Up Compaq Arena's Fate/City Forges Pact with Lakewood Church," *Houston Chronicle*, December 16, 2002.

[119] "America's Biggest Church Building Project/Lakewood Church Set to Transform Houston's Compaq Center," *Stewardship Solutions*, January 2005.

[120] Tara Dooley, "Arena of Worship/Church Brings Compaq Center into 'a New Era,'" *Houston Chronicle*, December 2, 2003.

[121] Ibid.

[122] "Church holds first services in former Compaq Center," KTRK-TV, http://abclocal.go.com/ktrk/story?section=local&id=3235773 (May 2006).

Chapter 20: Occupying the Promised Land

[123] Jennifer Dawson, "Compaq Center Gets Religion in Church," *Houston Business Journal*, January 2, 2004.

[124] Ibid.

[125] Jeremy Desel, "Osteen Previews New Home for Grand Vision," KHOU-TV, khou.com, July 11, 2005.

[126] Marianne Horton, "Lakewood Church Set to Open Doors," *H Texas Magazine*, http://www.htexas.com/feature.cfm?Story=451 (May 2006).

[127] Terry Pristin, "A Sports Arena Gets Religion," *The New York Times*, March 10, 2004.

[128] Susan Zahn, "Millions Tune-In to TBN to Watch Official Grand Opening of New Lakewood Church Center," TBN, July 19, 2005.

Chapter 21: Lakewood: The Largest Church in History

[129] Elmer L. Towns, *The Ten Largest Sunday Schools and What Makes Them Grow* (Grand Rapids, Michigan: Baker Book House, 1969).

[130] John N. Vaughan, *Megachurches & America's Cities: How Churches Grow* (Grand Rapids, Michigan: Baker Publishing Group, 1993).

[131] William Martin, "Prime Minister," *Texas Monthly*, August 2005.

Chapter 22: Criticisms and Concerns

[132] Douglas LeBlanc, "Thou Shalt Not Be Negative," *Christianity Today*, April 14, 2005.

[133] Dr. Jack Hayford, interview by Mark Mittleberg, "Awakened by the Spirit," *Outreach Magazine*, May/June, 2005.

Chapter 23: From Obscurity to Prominence

[134] John A. Zukowski, "The Joel Osteen Phenomenon," *The Newark (NJ) Express-Times*, July 8, 2005.

[135] William Martin, "Prime Minister," *Texas Monthly*, August 2005.

[136] Jennifer Mathieu, "Power House: What Does Lakewood Church and Its Pastor Joel Osteen Have That Most Mainline Denominations Don't? People. Lots of Them. And in an Assortment of Colors," *Houston Press*, April 4, 2002.

[137] Jean Christie, "10 Questions with Cindy Cruse-Ratcliff," http://www.integritymusic.com/new/artist/0502.html

[138] Lois Romano, "'The Smiling Preacher' Builds on Large Following," *The Washington Post*, January 30, 2005.

[139] Ian Brown, "Part 2: Supersize Thee," *The Toronto (ON) Globe and Mail*, March 5, 2005.

[140] William C. Symonds, "Earthly Empires: How evangelical churches are borrowing from the business playbook," *BusinessWeek*, May 23, 2005.

[141] http://www.thechurchreport.com/content/view/170/32/ (March 2006).

[142] http://www.thechurchreport.com/content/view/823/32/ (March 2006).

[143] John C. Roper, "At Lakewood, Goal Is to Be 'Good Stewards of God's Money,'" *Houston Chronicle*, July 24, 2005.

[144] Zukowski, "The Joel Osteen Phenomenon."

[145] John Leland, "A Church That Packs Them In, 16,000 at a Time," *The New York Times*, July 18, 2005.

[146] Zukowski, "The Joel Osteen Phenomenon."

[147] Steve Wilson, "Investigators: A Look at Evangelist Joel Osteen," KXYZ-TV 7, July 14, 2005.

[148] Steve Wilson, "Investigators: A Look at Evangelist Joel Osteen Part II," KXYZ-TV 7, July 15, 2005.

[149] Martin, "Prime Minister."

[150] Ibid.

[151] Ibid.

[152] Ibid.

ABOUT THE AUTHOR

Richard Young is a former educator, businessman, and pastor. The son of a Free Will Baptist pastor, Richard started preaching at fourteen and began pastoring at twenty. His family has a great heritage of preachers and pastors. There has been a member of his family in the ministry since 1876.

Richard received bachelor of arts and master of science degrees from Southern Nazarene University in Bethany, Oklahoma. He has completed the coursework for his doctorate of education at Oklahoma State University.

He served as vice president of academics at American Christian College and Seminary in Oklahoma City as well as dean of academics at Oklahoma Junior College. He also taught courses in business and administration. He was a trainer for Century 21 across the state of Oklahoma. Richard has been a writer all of his adult life. He has written training material for Century 21, collegiate self-study curriculum, and two textbooks. He has also written articles for both Christian and secular magazines and journals.

Richard lives in Oklahoma City, Oklahoma, with his wife, Brenda. They have been married for over thirty years and have three children and eight grandchildren.

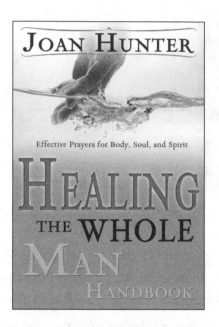

Healing the Whole Man Handbook:
Effective Prayers for Body, Soul, and Spirit
Joan Hunter

You can walk in divine health and healing. The secrets to God's words for healing and recovery are in this comprehensive, easy-to-follow guidebook containing powerful healing prayers that cover everything from abuse to yeast infections and everything in between.

Truly anointed with the gifts of healing, Joan Hunter has over thirty years of experience praying for the sick and brokenhearted and seeing them healed and set free. By following these step-by-step instructions and claiming God's promises, you can be healed, set free, and made totally whole—body, soul, and spirit!

ISBN: 978-0-88368-815-8 • Trade • 240 pages

www.whitakerhouse.com

A Healing Touch:
The Power of Prayer
Melanie Hemry

We all want prayers that move the hand of God. We want to be used and blessed and effective for the kingdom of God. But when someone says "intercessor," we balk, we run, we thank God that it's not our gift or our calling....But it is.

Melanie Hemry will challenge everything you ever believed about prayer. She will introduce you to a new kind of prayer—the soul-stirring, world-shaking, life-giving *prayer* that this world so desperately needs.

If you've been searching for God's presence, if you feel a deep need for unsaved souls, or even if you're just worried about the state of the world today, Melanie Hemry has the answer. As a former ICU nurse and prayer warrior, she is qualified to give you the heart transplant you need. You will not walk away from this book unchanged.

ISBN: 978-0-88368-780-2 • Trade • 192 pages

WHITAKER
HOUSE

www.whitakerhouse.com

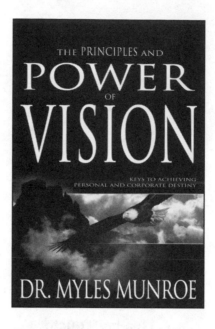

The Principles and Power of Vision
Dr. Myles Munroe

Whether you are a businessperson, a homemaker, a student, or a head of state, best-selling author Dr. Myles Munroe explains how you can make your dreams and hopes a living reality. Your success is not dependent on the state of the economy or what the job market is like. You do not need to be hindered by the limited perceptions of others or by a lack of resources. Discover time-tested principles that will enable you to fulfill your vision no matter who you are or where you come from.

You were not meant for a mundane or mediocre life. Revive your passion for living, pursue your dream, discover your vision—and find your true life.

ISBN: 978-0-88368-951-6 • Hardcover • 240 pages

WHITAKER
HOUSE

www.whitakerhouse.com

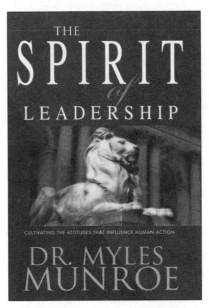

The Spirit of Leadership
Dr. Myles Munroe

Leaders may be found in boardrooms, but they may also be found in families, schools, and organizations of all kinds—anywhere people interact, nurture, create, or build. Contrary to popular opinion, leadership is not meant for an elite group of people who—by fate or accident—are allowed to be leaders while everyone else is consigned to being lifelong followers. After personally training thousands of leaders from around the world, best-selling author Dr. Myles Munroe reports that while all people possess leadership potential, many do not understand how to cultivate the leadership nature and how to apply it to their lives. Discover the unique attitudes that all effective leaders exhibit, how to eliminate hindrances to your leadership abilities, and how to fulfill your particular calling in life. With wisdom and power, Dr. Munroe reveals a wealth of practical insights that will move you from being a follower to becoming the leader you were meant to be!

ISBN: 978-0-88368-983-7 • Hardcover • 304 pages

www.whitakerhouse.com

It's Your Time:
Reclaim Your Territory for the Kingdom
Eddie Long

Have we, as believers, allowed the world to silence us? By slowly eroding our rights to free speech…by passing laws saying that marriage isn't necessarily between a man and a woman…that murder is okay… that it's wrong to display the Ten Commandments… Is this really equality for all, except for Christians?

Join Eddie Long in reclaiming what has been lost. He will inspire you to rise up, take authority, and boldly assert your power as a believer. Discover how to redefine your life's purpose and vision while you raise your children to be godly leaders. Speak up, Christians! Now is the time for our unified voice to be heard, to take a stand together, and to stand firm. It's our time.

ISBN: 978-0-88368-783-3 • Hardcover • 192 pages

WHITAKER
HOUSE

www.whitakerhouse.com